Forgotten Black Soldiers Who Served in White Regiments During the Civil War

Volume II

Juanita Patience Moss

HERITAGE BOOKS
2014

HERITAGE BOOKS

AN IMPRINT OF HERITAGE BOOKS, INC.

Books, CDs, and more—Worldwide

For our listing of thousands of titles see our website
at
www.HeritageBooks.com

Published 2014 by
HERITAGE BOOKS, INC.
Publishing Division
5810 Ruatan Street
Berwyn Heights, Md. 20740

Heritge Books by the author:

Anthracite Coal Art of Charles Edgar Patience

Battle of Plymouth, North Carolina (April 17–20, 1864): The Last Confederate Victory

Created to Be Free: A Historical Novel about One American Family

The Forgotten Black Soldiers in White Regiments During the Civil War, Revised Edition

The Forgotten Black Soldiers in White Regiments During the Civil War, Volume II

Tell Me Why Dear Bennett: Memoirs of Bennett College Belles, Class of 1924–2012

Tell Me Why Dear Bennett: Memoirs of Bennett College Belles, Volume II

International Standard Book Numbers
Paperbound: 978-0-7884-5540-7
Clothbound: 978-0-7884-9097-2

"Forgotten Black Soldiers" is a very important facet of Civil War History that is rarely looked upon. A must read for Civil War Scholars and Historians, sharing the many stories of soldiers that participated in the war of the rebellion. The author does a superb job in bringing this subject to light. Highly recommend."

Y'r Most Humble & Ob't Servant,
--Charles (Ben) Hawley, Private, B Company, Secretary, Treasurer, 54th Mass. Vol. Inf. Reg., Washington, D.C.

*"Historic Blenheim has been so fortunate to have had return visits by Dr. Juanita Patience Moss, who has presented her incredible story of "**Forgotten Black Soldiers Who Served in White Regiments During the Civil War.**" Her pursuit of a family story turned into an amazing odyssey of previously unrecognized information about many black Civil War soldiers. Her book is impeccably researched and documented while holding fast to her personal journey."*
--**Andrea J. Loewenwarter,** Historic Resources Specialist, Historic Blenheim, City of Fairfax, Virginia

"A few years ago after researching and locating an ancestor of African descent who had served as a soldier in a Pennsylvania regiment during the Civil War, and his name was not engraved on the memorial wall of the African American Civil War Memorial in Washington, D.C., the author embarked on a remarkable research journey with a specific purpose of locating and documenting hundreds of others who were missing from the pages of history.

Dr. Juanita Patience Moss wandered off into a wonderful region of Civil War history that had been overlooked or ignored by scholars and establishment historians.

There are many untold facts related to Civil War history, many probably will remain dormant forever; however, Dr. Moss has contributed greatly to uncovering a very important missing link: the names, units and other important data on patriotic individuals of African descent who also contributed to making this nation what it is today, a Union victory."
--Bennie J. McCrae, military history researcher; Trotwood, Ohio

"In her second major publication, Dr. Moss continues her tireless pursuit of long-neglected records of African-American troops who served the North during the Civil War. The book is an excellent resource for Black History studies, genealogical research, and personal enlightenment."
-- **Rosalie Miller**, Librarian, Edenton, Chowan County, North Carolina

"Being the Historian of the 1st Alabama Cavalry US Volunteers, I was surprised to locate sixteen Black soldiers who served in this regiment. I was also surprised to find my great great grandfather Andrew Ferrier McWhirter and his son, George Washington McWhirter buried in the Nashville National Cemetery, since they were from Alabama.

I heard in 2008 about Dr. Juanita Moss who was researching her ancestor who had served in the 103rd PA Infantry. I contacted her to share my research on the sixteen Blacks in the 1st Alabama Cavalry, USV and thus began a wonderful relationship. I have gained a special friend in Dr. Moss due to "our" research.

I shared with her how I ordered tombstones for the unmarked graves of Privates Simon West in Cleveland, Ohio, as well as Amos McKinney in Decatur, Alabama, and John Read Porter in Huntsville, Alabama, where the First Alabama Cavalry USV Re-enactors held Memorial Services.

Dr. Moss has diligently researched not only her family, but also other forgotten Black Civil War soldiers. Although it was a tiring exercise, as is most all research of Black people, she found what she was looking for and has written her second book to help other descendants find their ancestors' names in print."
--**Glenda McWhirter Todd,** Author of ***First Alabama Cavalry USA - Homage to Patriotism and Unionists in the Heart of Dixie, Volumes I, II, III, & IV; Heartbreak of a Civil War Widow***

"Moss' book is refreshing and incredibly well documented Her passion to illuminate, research, and preserve the experiences of forgotten black soldiers and the roles they played during the Civil War is a great achievement. This inspiring work is an exceptional piece of American History."
--**Peggy Allen Towns**, author of ***Duty Driven***; Decatur, Alabama

"Many stories of African Americans in the Civil War were suppressed and falsified. One of those stories was the story of African American soldiers who served in other than the United States Colored Troops.

Thanks to the work of Dr. Juanita Patience Moss that story is part of an informed and intelligent study of the Civil War. As a Civil War historian, I am very grateful for the work that Dr. Moss has done. Her work is of great importance to those who seek a complete and accurate history. Though not an historian by training, she has trained many historians.

Dr. Juanita Patience Moss has contributed significantly to the study of African Americans in the Civil War; thus she has contributed significantly to the study of American history."

Semper Fi

Hari Jones, Curator, AFRICAN AMERICAN CIVIL WAR MUSEUM, Washington, D.C.

"Spirit of Freedom" Monument
AFRICAN AMERICAN CIVIL WAR MUSEUM, Washington, D.C.

This book is dedicated to each Black soldier who served in any capacity during the Civil War.

"Once let the black man get upon his person the brass letters 'U.S.,' let him get an eagle on his button, and a musket on his shoulder and bullets in his pocket, and there is no power on earth which can deny that he has earned the right to citizenship in the United States."

Frederick Douglass

TABLE OF CONTENTS

AFRICAN AMERICAN CIVIL WAR MUSEUM
1925 Vermont Avenue NW
Washington, D.C. 20001
(Photo Courtesy of Reba N. Burruss-Barnes)

PHOTOGRAPHS AND DOCUMENTS

ACKNOWLEDGEMENTS

Special thanks to each person seeking to remember what was heretofore forgotten. Thanks for your contributions to the two volumes of ***Forgotten Black Soldiers Who Served in White Regiments During the Civil War.***

Since 1998 when I began to research Black Civil War soldiers, many persons have provided me with support in various ways. The following is a list of persons who have especially helped me to gather information for Volume II:

Sheila M. Bourelly, collateral relative of Martin Scott of the 19th Indiana Regiment.

Joan Bryant, associate professor, African American Studies Department, Syracuse University.

Reba N. Burruss-Barnes, publicist-REBAssociates and photographer.

John Carter, Civil War historian.

Willie Cooper, author of ***The Forgotten Legacy: Black Soldiers and Sailors Who Fought in The Civil War, 1862-1866.***

Kelly A. Farquhar, historian, Montgomery County Department of History and Archives, Old Courthouse, Fonda, N.Y.

Robert Farrell, Civil War historian.

Ruth Fulton, 103rd Pennsylvania Volunteers historian.

Charles "Ben" Hawley, Civil War re-enactor.

Hari Jones, curator of the African American Civil War Museum in Washington, D.C.

Fred Kligge, whose 2nd great grandfather served in Co. G of the 16th Connecticut volunteers and was captured at Plymouth, N.C. He shared copies of his ancestor's letters to his wife and father back home.

Andrea Loewenwarter, curator of Blenheim House, Fairfax, Virginia.

Bennie McRae, webmaster of "Lest We Forget."

Rosalie Miller, former librarian of Shepard-Pruden Memorial Library, Edenton, N.C.
Nadia Orton, historian and genealogist, African American cemeteries of Tidewater, Virginia and North Carolina.
Sandra Panzitta, research assistant, Luzerne County Historical Society, Wilkes-Barre, Penna.
Vivian Fox Porche, great-granddaughter of Pvt. William Fox 2nd Michigan Cavalry.
Maia Porche great-great-granddaughter of Pvt. William Fox, 2nd Michigan Cavalry.
Geoffrey Satter, Civil War historian.
Peggy Sawyer-Williams, great granddaughter of Pvt. Aquilla Lett 13th Michigan Infantry Co K.
Craig Scott, publisher, president and CEO of Heritage Books, Inc.
Rev. Wylhelme Ragland, retired United Methodist pastor in Decatur, Alabama.
Dr. Frank Smith, director of the African American Civil War Museum in Washington, D.C.
Sharon Johnson Swan, computer consultant.
The late Harry Thompson, renowned curator of Port O' Plymouth Museum.
The late William Gladstone, consummate collector of Black Civil War soldiers' photographs.
Glenda McWhither Todd, 1st Alabama Cavalry historian, author of ***Heartbreak of a Civil War Widow: Including Harper Ancestry to 1500's: 1st Alabama Cavalry, USV Family vs. CSA.***
Peggy Allen Towns, former congressional aide to the Honorable Parker Griffith, author of ***Duty Driven: The Plight of North Alabama's African Americans During the Civil War.***
Ethel Washington, history program coordinator of the Union County Office of Cultural and Heritage Affairs, author of ***Union County's Black Soldiers and Sailors of the Civil War.***

Thanks to each person who has helped in any way with the discovery of the names of Black soldiers who have been forgotten for over 150 years.

PREFACE

The search for the names of Blacks who served in the Union Army during the Civil War is an ongoing project. Some reasons are that many names have been hidden, or forgotten, or ignored, or simply dismissed as not being important.

Not until this present time has there been such an opportunity for the inquiring to search the multitudinous amounts of information in census and military records, as well as birth and death records. Descendants today searching for ancestors no longer have to rely solely on what was recorded in the family Bible or via oral history. Many questions may never be answered, but those that can, might possibly be.

Such it is with my family whose first known ancestor is Crowder Patience, a slave born in North Carolina (circa 1846). Due to his service during the Civil War, a heretofore forgotten historical fact was brought to my attention in 1998. The fact is that Blacks had served in white regiments, too, and not just in the segregated ones.

Volume II is a continuation of my research since the 2008 publication of the revised version of ***Forgotten Black Soldiers Who Served in White Regiments During the Civil War*** first published in 2004. A major purpose is to encourage other descendants to discover their ancestors whose contributions to the Civil War have been forgotten by historians, also.

My original research was focused mainly on Black cooks such as my ancestor had been. On their military records, those particular soldiers are racially identified because under General Orders No. 323,[1] Blacks were allowed to enlist as undercooks. Once mustered in, many became blacksmiths, farriers, wagoners/teamsters, saddlers, hospital stewards, and even buglers.

In order to be appreciative of the contributions of Black Civil War soldiers, all of their roles should be studied. On that note, I have divided them into seven groups with possibly an eighth for women serving under General Orders No. 323.

The seven groups provided the basis for my C-Span Book TV presentation on 23 September 2013 and are as follows:

1. New England "patriots"[2] who served as "independents" without rank.

2. Fully mustered-in Black soldiers prior to the Emancipation Proclamation.[3]

3. Black regiments organized without presidential or congressional permission.

4. Blacks in mixed-race regiments both prior to and after the Emancipation Proclamation.

5. Enlistees under General Orders No. 143[4] after the Emancipation Proclamation had been signed. The first four Colored units, the three Massachusetts and one Conn. regiments, were allowed to keep their state identification.

6. United States Colored Troops (U.S.C.T.)[5]

7. Undercooks enlisted under General Orders No. 323.

Again using those categories as a basis, I have written Volume II to include the contributions of several Black soldiers and to provide directions for discovering even more. Possibly, readers may find that not only had one of their ancestors served in the Civil War, they may find, also, that he was a decorated hero. That is exactly what happened to a descendant of Medal of Honor recipient Pvt. Bruce Anderson of the 142nd New York Infantry.

CHAPTER 1

DIFFICULTIES WITH FINDING FACTS

C | 38 | Wis.

Isaac Collins

Appears with rank of Cook

Muster and Descriptive Roll of a Detachment of U. S. Vols. forwarded

for the 38 Reg't Wisconsin. Inf. Roll dated

Madison Wis Sept. 19, 1864

Where born Wake N.C.

Age 44 y'rs; occupation Farmer

When enlisted Aug. 6, 1864

Where enlisted Friendship, Wis.

For what period enlisted 1 years.

Eyes Black; hair Black

Complexion Black; height 5 ft. 6 in.

When mustered in Sept. 19, 1864

Where mustered in Madison, Wis.

Bounty paid $ .... 100; due $ 100 100

Where credited ....

Company to which assigned ....

Remarks Credited to Town of Trenton Dodge Co. 4" Dis. Wis.

Book mark: ....

Randall
Copyist.

(889)

Pvt. Isaac Collins
38th Wisconsin Infantry Co. C

Included in this second volume are several different kinds of Civil War military documents for readers to see how pertinent information was recorded, such as the physical characteristics of the soldier, as seen on Pvt. Isaac Collins' record. Place of birth and names of family members may be found on pension applications. Obituaries mentioning military burials prove those Black men indeed were bona fide soldiers. Collection of concrete information, therefore, can be as simple as locating gravestones, or as complex as poring through military records and pension applications.

Families such as mine are blessed to have copies of our ancestor's discharge information. Other families may have an oral history treasured for generations, but who now are looking for verification. In other families, however, the stories were never told for diverse reasons. Simply, the degradation of slavery was something to be forgotten. Never to be discussed. In addition, many children of former slaves did not want to hear anything about slavery.[6] It was much too shameful.

Searchers will discover that one of the difficulties they will encounter is that in many instances, names were spelled differently for the same man on military records due to the fact that most Blacks were illiterate. So the recruiter spelled what he thought he was hearing. For instance my ancestor's surname was spelled "Pacien," "Patient," "Pacient," on different military reports, and on his tombstone "Patience."

Oftentimes military records provided aliases such as for teamster August Amon/Amand, who served in the 2nd Missouri Light Artillery. Through the years some surnames were changed by just a single letter like James M. Angel/Angle.

An additional example is the comparison of the surnames of Burk Grixby and Martin Grigsby who both served in the 9th Illinois Infantry. Since relatives often joined the same unit for both safety in numbers and for camaraderie, the two may have been related. In such a case, descendants mistakenly may dismiss one man because of the difference in spelling, when, in fact, he might be the actual sought-after ancestor.

Another difficulty relates to unknown burial sites. In some cases when soldiers died in battle, their families had no idea where their loved ones were buried. They simply had not returned home.

On the other hand, some veterans may have lived for many years after the war had ended, as had Pvt. Thomas Patience of the 5th Massachusetts Cavalry. He had returned home to Edenton, North Carolina, and lived there until 1929. His death certificate states only that he was buried in Chowan County, but just where is not known.

Still another problem is that many soldiers had identical names and if a middle initial were not included, names listed more than once may actually have been for the same person. Or maybe not. For instance, over 100 William Williams served with the United States Colored Troops (U.S.C.T.). [7] To know with certainty which of those names are duplications, one would have to study each soldier's records stored at the National Archives in Washington, D.C.

Complicating matters even further, soldiers often served in more than one company, especially when numbers had to be adjusted due to illness, death, and desertions. Consequently, names may have been counted more than once.

To further add to the confusion, some soldiers served in different regiments in the same state, such as Pvt. Philip Ackerman who served in both the 5th and the 7th New Jersey Infantry.[8] Finally, others even served in several different states as had Pvt. Joseph Brandt who was in both the 1st New Jersey Infantry and the 29th Pennsylvania Infantry.[9]

Some soldiers might even have changed branches by leaving the Army to join the Navy or the Artillery. Such an example is Pvt. Edmund Voorhees who had enlisted in the 14th New Jersey Infantry Co. C, but later became a sailor.[10]

Although the names of Black cooks who enlisted under General Orders No. 323 are found at the end of rosters recorded in regimental histories, the problem is that every regiment does not have a published history. Some rosters, however, can be studied on the Internet, but not all, requiring a trip to Washington, D.C.

There is a process in place for going about that, however, for time is of the essence. For one reason, the National Archives in Washington, D.C., are not open on Saturdays when many out-of-town researchers might want to pay the Nation's Capitol a visit.

Consequently, on crowded weekdays one must arrive quite early in order to make the most of the day. Even though I am just a Metro ride away, one of my problems has been in not arriving at the Archives early enough to submit the information I needed to be pulled by a staff member. A definite schedule is in place and if one should miss a pull, then he/she has to wait for the next one.

Three years ago when I arrived just minutes too late, I retreated to my favorite spot—the Library where I could research while watching the wall clock's hands inch forward ever so slowly. My appointed time for the Research Room was scheduled for 2:00 p.m. and I had over an hour to wait.

Because one cannot take anything into the Research Room, close to 1:45 p.m. I began to gather my belongings to store in a locker. Suddenly I felt the sensation of a strong shake. Just one. The librarian and I simultaneously exclaimed, "What was that?"

As we were commiserating, an employee came into the Library to announce that there has been an earthquake and that we were to evacuate the building immediately.

It was 1:51 p.m. on the 23rd of August 2011.

CHAPTER 2

C-SPAN BOOK TV PRESENTATION

Filmed on 23 September 2013 at the Blenheim House, Fairfax, Virginia
Andrea Loewenwarter, Curator

Because of a connection I had with the Blenheim House, a museum in Fairfax, Virginia, I was invited to be the guest author during the "Fall for the Books," an annual book fair sponsored by the George Mason University in Fairfax County in Northern Virginia. Only two days before the presentation, I was asked if I would consent to being filmed and then aired by C-Span. Of course, I was delighted.

The presentation was a PowerPoint which was not filmed in its entirety since some slides were not shown, but all of my words were heard. I have chosen some pertinent excerpts of the presentation for this second volume concerning Black Civil War soldiers.

http://c-spanvideo.org/program/315160-1

"BLACK SOLDIERS DURING THE CIVIL WAR"

When the Civil War erupted on 12 April 1861, ninety-day state militias organized to protect Washington, D.C. Enthusiastic Black men hurried to enlist, but were rejected due to a Federal law of 1792 forbidding Colored men to bear arms in the Army, even though some had served in both the Revolutionary War and War of 1812.

In spite of the law, a number of New Englanders known as "patriots" managed to serve the Union without rank, in what may designated as a first category of Black soldiers during the Civil War.

William Henry Johnson

Such a "patriot" was a Norwich, Connecticut, resident, William Henry Johnson, born in Alexandria, Virginia.[11]

After attempting to join the local regiment when it responded to the first call for state militia troops, he was refused because of his race. He was, however, accepted into the 2nd Connecticut Volunteer Infantry as an "independent" without rank.

After the completed duration of three months, he enlisted in the 8th Connecticut Volunteer Infantry, participating on 21 July 1861 in the First Battle of Bull Run, as it was called by the Union, but Manassas by the Confederacy.

Seven months later William Henry Johnson participated in the "Burnside Expedition" that captured Roanoke Island, N.C. In his autobiography he wrote that other New England Black "patriots" or "independents" were on Roanoke Island, too. Unknown is the number of "patriots" who served the Union long before Blacks officially were allowed to become bona-fide soldiers.

Before bad health forced him to leave the military, William Henry Johnson had written articles for the Boston *Pine and Palm* paper.[12] He described what took place on Roanoke Island. In later years he became an important Black personality in Albany, N.Y.[13]

During the early months of the war, a second category would consist of fully mustered-in Black soldiers such as Pvt. James Reeder of the 1st Rhode Island Light Infantry. He, also, fought at Bull Run. Again, how many others were in this category is not known, thus providing another project for a future researcher.

Black Civil War Soldiers 1861-1865

Name:	**James Reeder**
Side:	Union
Regiment State/Origin:	Rhode Island
Regiment Name:	1 Rhode Island L. Art'y.
Regiment Name Expanded:	1st Regiment, Rhode Island Light Artillery
Company:	G
Film Number:	M555 roll 6

14

As the war progressed, Southern territory under Union control would provide the largest number of Black soldiers. Seeking the freedom, safety and employment offered behind the Federal lines, Blacks absconded in droves—alone or with families.

Gen. Benjamin Butler coined the name "contraband"[15] for the runaway slaves since they were seized enemy property just like cotton, machinery, or other goods. Due to the rapidly growing number of contrabands, the 1st Confiscation Act was signed on 6 August 1861. It authorized the seizing by Union forces of any Confederate property, and that property included slaves.

The 2nd Confiscation Act was passed eleven months later. It freed slaves of owners in rebellion against the United States. At the same time the Military Act was passed. It empowered the President to use those freed slaves in any capacity in the Army such as "for the purpose of construction of entrenchments, or performing camp duty, or any labor, or any military or naval service."[16] Those three acts would aid the growing movement towards emancipation of the slaves.

Even so, despite pleas from northern abolitionists, President Abraham Lincoln continued to refuse Blacks in the Union Army. Regardless, unofficial volunteer regiments formed from the Louisiana Native Guards who were Creole French speaking "free persons of color." Organized originally as militia in 1861 to serve the Confederacy, they never were accepted into the Confederate Army.

After Gen. Benjamin Butler's occupation of New Orleans in April 1862, they became the *Corps d'Afrique* [17] with 10% of the Louisiana men joining the Union Army, becoming the 1st, 2nd, and 3rd Louisiana Native Guards. They later had the distinction of being the first three Black units officially mustered into the Union Army.

Four months later in August 1862, another unofficial regiment, the 1st Kansas Colored Infantry [18] was organized, consisting primarily of fugitive slaves from Arkansas and Missouri. Their performance in a Missouri raid helped dispel the notion that Blacks were unable or unwilling to fight. Later it would become the 4th official Black regiment.

Also, without presidential or congressional authorization, another regiment composed of ex-slaves, the 1st South Carolina was raised by Generals David Hunter and Rufus Saxton, and later became the 5th official Black regiment.[19] These five unofficial regiments form a third category of Black Civil War soldiers.

During the summer of 1862, President Lincoln was still adamantly refusing Black men in the regular Army even though the Black abolitionist and orator Frederick Douglass kept pleading with him.

Douglass and other leaders viewed Black military service as an opportunity to win a Union victory and for Blacks to gain equality and rights as citizens.

<u>Frederick Douglass</u>
(Library of Congress)

His prophetic words stated: ***"Once let the black man get upon his person the brass letters 'U.S.,' let him get an eagle on his button, and a musket on his shoulder and bullets in his pocket, and there is no power on earth which can deny that he has earned the right to citizenship in the United States."***[20]

Not until the war had dragged on for two long bitter years with mounting casualties and desertions, as well as an unsuccessful draft would the President finally relent. First, though, he had to sign a formal Emancipation Proclamation. Finally, it was issued on 1 January 1863, freeing all slaves in rebellious states with the exception of those in areas already under Union control. It did not free, however, the slaves in Maryland, Delaware, Kansas, and Missouri due to the President's fear of losing those slave-holding border-states.

Secondly, the Proclamation declared that Blacks could officially be received into the United States Army. Consequently, many Colored men immediately took advantage of the new ruling and joined mixed-race regiments, which created a fourth category. Since no racial identification is registered in military records, again the number in this category cannot be determined. One such soldier, though, was Medal of Honor Bruce Anderson, a member of the 142nd New York Infantry. He is buried in the Greenhill Cemetery in Amsterdam, New York.

CHAPTER 3

MIXED RACE REGIMENTS

The fourth category contains not only such identifiably Colored men like Bruce Anderson and the Fort Ann, New York Jackson brothers Pvts. Virgil, Damion, Abner, Alexander, and, their half-brother William Lamb, [21] but also light-skinned Colored men scattered in volunteer white regiments. Pvt. Aquilla Lett was one such soldier.

Pvt. Aquilla Lett
13th Michigan Infantry
(courtesy of Peggy Sawyer Williams)

At the age of thirty-five he joined the 13th Michigan Infantry that organized near his hometown in Michigan where his family was well known. A photograph of Aquilla Lett with several of his military records were mailed to me by his great granddaughter, Peggy Sawyer-Williams, after she had read my first publication about forgotten Black soldiers in white regiments.

Moving from Meigs Township in southern Ohio, Aquilla Lett had settled his family on a farm in Arlington Township, Van Buren County, Michigan. During the Civil War, with other Colored men from the area of Paw Paw, Michigan, thirty-five -year old Pvt. Lett answered the call for volunteers. His regiment marched during the winter of 1864-1865 from Chattanooga, Tennessee; Savannah, Georgia; and ended at the nation's capitol. When he mustered out in Washington, D.C., on 8 June 1865, he received a clothing allowance of $29.00 and $100.00 bounty pay.[22]

Serving in the same regiment with Pvt. Aquilla Lett was Pvt. Hopkins West (listed as a Mulatto on the 1860 census) who testified in 1887 on Aquilla Lett's behalf for a pension:

"The first I noticed of Mr. Aquilla Lett complaining was while laying in the swamp at Savannah, Georgia. He was excused from duty or work on the fort. He having the piles and rheumatism. Piles caused by hard marching and the rheumatism caused by laying exposed to the weather in the swamp. And he was complaining at different times on the march from Savannah to Raleigh and to Washington." [23]

Peggy Sawyer-Williams also provided the name of another Michigan soldier who was drafted as a substitute from Grand Rapids, Michigan. Eighteen-year-old Pvt. Benjamin F. Guy served in the 16th Michigan Infantry Co. F. [24]

Name:	**Benjamin F. Guy**
Side:	Union
Regiment State/Origin:	Michigan
Regiment Name:	16 Michigan Infantry
Regiment Name Expanded:	16th Regiment, Michigan Infantry
Company:	F
Rank In:	Private
Rank In Expanded:	Private
Rank Out:	Private
Rank Out Expanded:	Private
Film Number:	M545 roll 17

25

Vivian Fox Porche and great great granddaughter Maia Porche shared information about their ancestor, Kentucky born Pvt. William Dudley Fox. He was drafted into the 2nd Michigan Cavalry Co. F on 14 November 1863. The regiment was mustered out 17 August 1865 in Macon, Georgia. [26]

Another name was sent from Sheila Bourelly, a collateral relative of Pvt. Martin Scott who had been married to her great-great-aunt. Born in Raleigh, N.C., Martin Scott was residing in Owen County, Indiana, when the Civil War erupted. Most of the other Black men from his vicinity joined the 28th U.S. Colored Regiment; however, due to his light complexion, he was able to enlist in the 19th Indiana Regiment as a white man.

Pvt. Martin Scott was wounded at the Battle of the Wilderness fought on May 5 through the 7th of 1864 in central Virginia with 18,400 casualties. After his capture he was sent to Andersonville Prison where he was confined for many months. Nine soldiers in the 19th Indiana Regiment died there. Fortunately Martin Scott was not among that number. Later he was quoted as saying that if his captors ***"had known that I was a black man, I would have been a dead man."*** [27]

Andersonville Prison records state that he was a private in Company I, was held there and survived, later being moved to Camp Lawton at Millen, Georgia, on 11 November 1864. When 90 year-old Martin Scott died in April 1918, he was considered to be one of oldest citizens of Owen County, Indiana. [28]

Wilson Bruce Evans and his brother, residents of Oberlin, Ohio, built a large red brick home in 1854-56 at 33 East Vine Street. The two free-born Blacks had been carpenters and furniture makers in North Carolina prior to their move to the North. Because of evidence that they had broken the Fugitive Slave Law of 1850 by secretly aiding in the transportation of a slave to Canada, they were incarcerated with others for eighty-four days. [29]

During the Civil War, Pvt. Wilson Bruce Evans was another Colored man who chose to pass as white in order to enlist in the United States Army. After the war ceased, he returned to his family in Oberlin where he continued in his successful carpentry business. On 7 April 1998, the Wilson Bruce Evans House in Oberlin, Ohio, was designated a National Historic Landmark. [30]

On Wednesday, 4 January 2012, Carol Kammen wrote in the *New York History: Historical News and Views From the Empire State* that she had read an obituary from 1865 that led her to investigate the life of Pvt. Ira T. Brum. He had been a member of the 185th New York Volunteers Co. F which participated in the siege of Petersburg and was part of the Appomattox Campaign. Unfortunately, soon after his company was mustered out, thirty year-old Pvt. Ira Brum died. His obituary stated that he was the only "*colored man in his company.*" [31]

Pvt. Asberry Allen, born in North Carolina and reared in Illinois, is listed on censuses as a Mulatto. As did many others like himself, he crossed racial barriers by moving and changing his name to enlist in the 142nd New York Infantry Co. D. When his widow America Allen was applying for a widow's pension in 1890 after his death in 1888, she did not know the names of his regiment or company. A lawyer discovered that according to military records, no Asberry Allen was found in any regiment, but an Asher Allen was. On 6 July 1892 two affidavits were marked by persons testifying that Asher and Asberry were indeed the same man. Eventually, America did receive an $8.00 per month pension.[32]

The following information regarding Pvt. William Appo is verbatum from historians John Carter and Joseph Romeo.[33]

"William Appo was born in New York City about 1842, but later raised in Philadelphia. He must have been with his father in North Elba, Essex County, N.Y. in the autumn of 1859, for he witnessed a deed for him. This compiler has been unable to determine his whereabouts in the 1860 census. When the Civil War came along, he volunteered. On Septermber 15, 1861, was mustered in at Albany, N.Y. He belonged to Co. I, 30 Reg't N.Y Infantry. On February 2, 1862, he was promoted to the rank of corporal. He was killed in action at the Second Battle of Bull Run, August 30, 1862, and buried on the Bull Run Battlefield.

The Appos were of mixed ancestry; the progenitor of the family, St. John Appo, allegedly came from Pondicherry, India; his wife was allegedly white. The family worshipped in Philadelphia's St. Thomas African Protestant Episcopal Church. The children, including the father of William above, were part of Philadelphia's 'colored society.'"

Pvt. Ephraim Pierce served in the 48th N.Y. Infantry Co. F. His wife's application for a widow's pension was sent to me by his great-great niece, Joan Bryant, Associate Professor of African American Studies Department, Syracuse University. The document includes information concerning his racial identity:

"I do not know when Ephraim Pierce went to the war. He and his uncle Charles Pierce went away together.

They went away because their people did not want them to enlist.

No, I do not know if Ephraim and Charles served in the same regiment or not. I had the original discharge of my husband which I will give to you for use in this examination.

Yes, my husband had a pension when he died on August 29, 1913. I never met any of my husband's commanders of the war except Charles Pierce who knows all about him.

Yes, my husband told me that he went to New York and enlisted in a white regiment. His parents were colored people, but his father and himself were both fair skinned men and unless you knew you could not tell my husband from a white man." [34]

Another soldier of considerable interest is Pvt. Thomas Eston Hemings, son of Madison Hemings, son of Sally Hemings of Monticello. According to his Volunteer Enlistment paper, he was mustered into the service of the United States for one year or during the war from the date of enlistment in the 178th Regiment of Ohio Infantry on the 17th day of August, 1864 at Hillsboro, Ohio.

VOLUNTEER ENLISTMENT.

STATE OF Ohio — TOWN OF New Lexington

I, Thomas Hemings, born in Ross Co in the State of Ohio, aged twenty one years, and by occupation a Laborer, DO HEREBY ACKNOWLEDGE to have volunteered this Sixteenth day of August, 1864, to serve as a **Soldier** in the **Army of the United States of America**, for the period of ~~THREE~~ one YEARS, unless sooner discharged by proper authority: Do also agree to accept such bounty, pay, rations, and clothing, as are, or may be, established by law for volunteers. And I, Thomas Hemings, do solemnly swear, that I will bear true faith and allegiance to the ***United States of America***, and that I will serve them honestly and faithfully against all their enemies or opposers whomsoever; and that I will observe and obey the orders of the President of the United States, and the orders of the officers appointed over me, according to the Rules and Articles of War.

Sworn and subscribed to, at New Lexington O. this 16 day of August 1864, Before F M Doggate, 2nd Lieut Recruiting Officer — Thomas his mark Hemings

I CERTIFY, ON HONOR, That I have carefully examined the above-named Volunteer, agreeably to the General Regulations of the Army, and that, in my opinion, he is free from all bodily defects and mental infirmity, which would in any way disqualify him from performing the duties of a soldier.

David Noble
Surgeon Board of Enrollment
6th Dist O

I CERTIFY, ON HONOR, That I have minutely inspected the Volunteer Thomas Hemings previously to his enlistment, and that he was entirely sober when enlisted; that, to the best of my judgment and belief, he is of lawful age; and that, in accepting him as duly qualified to perform the duties of an able-bodied soldier, I have strictly observed the Regulations which govern the recruiting service. This soldier has brown eyes, dark hair, dark complexion, is 5 feet 7 3/4 inches high.

F M Doggate
Regiment of Ohio Volunteers,
2nd Lieut & RECRUITING OFFICER.

(A. G. O. No. 74 & 76.)

Mustered into the service of the United States, for ~~three~~ one years or during the war, from date of enlistment, in Company ___ 176 Regiment of Ohio Infantry Volunteers, on the 17 day of August, 1864, at Hillsboro O

Capt ... Mustering Officer

Pvt. Thomas Hemings Volunteer Enlistment

ANDERSONVILLE NHS
Civil War Resource File
Information Sheet

Instructions: Complete the appropriate sections, recording all requested information available. Place additional information in the "Remarks" section.

Personal Information

Last Name: Hemmings First/Middle Name: Thomas Eston
Regiment/Ship: 175TH OHIO VOL INF Company: H (E) Rank: PVT
Date of Enlistment: 8/16/1864 Age at Enlistment: 26
Alternate Name 1: ____ Alternate Name 2: ____

NOTE: ORIGINALLY FORMED AS 178TH OVI, WHICH BECAME 175TH OVI (Co BY G.O. # 243 (A.G. of OHIO) ISSUED 8/19/1864.

Union Personnel

Known Camp Sumter Prisoner: ____ Reported Camp Sumter Prisoner: ✓
Capture Date: 11/24/1864 Place of Capture: BLOCK House #6 NEAR COLUMBIA TN.
Parole Date: ____ Parole Location: ____
Died at Camp Sumter: ____ Reported to Have Died at Camp Sumter: ✓
Death Date: ____ Cause of Death: ____ Grave #: ____
Others Prisons Held: ____

Confederate Personnel

Stationed at Camp Sumter: ____ Reported Stationed at Camp Sumter: ____
Dates of Duty at Camp Sumter: ____
Prisoner of War?: ____ Prisons Held: ____
Capture Date: ____ Place of Capture: ____
Parole Date: ____ Parole Location: ____
Death Date: ____ Cause of Death: ____
Grave Location: ____ Grave #: ____

Information Contained in File (Place a Check Mark for all that apply)

Compiled Military Service Record: ✓
Memorandum from Prisoner of War Records only: ____
Pension Files: ____ Application Only?: ____
Additional Information?: ✓ Type of Info: newspaper articles

Remarks: * reported to be the grandson of Thomas Jefferson

<u>Andersonville Prison Report</u>

"Remarks reported to be the grandson of Thomas Jefferson"

A newspaper article, "Jefferson's Kin May Have Died at Prison," written by Alia Bear was published in the *Americus Times Records* on Sunday, 8 November 1998.[35] Also, in *The Memoirs of Madison Hemings*, the father stated that his son, Pvt. Thomas Eston Hemings, had died at Andersonville Prison,[36] albeit the actual site is not known.

Madison also stated that after the death on 4 July 1826 of his father Thomas Jefferson, he and younger brother Eston left Monticello with their mother Sally Hemings to live in Charlottesville, Virginia. Both sons had been freed by Thomas Jefferson, but their mother was not. She would live until 1835 after which time the sons moved to Chillicothe, Ohio. [37]

The two sons had married and were rearing families in southern Ohio when the 1850 Fugitive Slave Law [38] was passed. It allowed slave owners to go throughout the United States to retrieve their human property. Consequently, every Colored person anywhere and everywhere was in danger of being kidnapped, whether slave or free.[39] Even the "free-papers" they carried might not be honored. In Ohio, therefore, where the two Hemings families had settled, runaway slaves as well as free-born Blacks were in danger.

Consider that prior to the Civil War, a newspaper writer mentioned to Eston Hemings that he had seen a bronze bust of Thomas Jefferson in Washington, D.C. and that Eston looked just like the third president. Eston had replied that his mother had been Thomas Jefferson's slave and that she was never married. [40]

Might the Fugitive Slave Law be the reason Eston Hemings chose to move his family from Ohio to Madison, Wisconsin, in 1852? There he changed their surname to Jefferson and passed into the white world. At the time of the move, Eston Jefferson's oldest son John Wayles Jefferson was fifteen years old. Unfortunately, his father would die a short time later.

During the Civil War, John Wayles Jefferson as a colonel led the 8th Wisconsin Infantry. The same reporter who had observed the resemblance years before between President Thomas Jefferson and Eston Hemings had an opportunity to talk with the young colonel who begged that his race not be revealed and the reporter complied. [41]

Name:	**John W. Jefferson** **[*John Wayles Jefferson*]**
Side:	Union
Regiment State/Origin:	Wisconsin
Regiment Name:	8 Wisconsin Infantry.
Regiment Name Expanded:	8th Regiment, Wisconsin Infantry
Company:	F&S
Rank In:	Major
Rank In Expanded:	Major
Rank Out:	Colonel
Rank Out Expanded:	Colonel
Film Number:	M559 roll 15

Col. John Wayles Jefferson [42]
8th Wisconsin Infantry

A third Sally Hemings' grandson served in the Civil War, also. He was Eston's other son, Beverly Frederick Jefferson, who was a private in the 1st Wisconsin Infantry, Co. E. [43] The tradition of naming children after family members is quite evident in the Hemings/Jefferson families. For instance, Thomas Eston Hemings was named after his uncle Eston Hemings who changed his surname to Jefferson. Son Beverly Jefferson was named after his uncle Beverly Hemings who after leaving Monticello entered the White world.

CHAPTER 4

HONORING CIVIL WAR VETERANS

Secrets, like those of the Hemings descendants, have been hidden likewise by many other families for generations, even to the present time. Race being such an issue due to the South's "peculiar institution"[44] and the "one drop policy,"[45] hiding one's mixed-identity was far more important to the success of the future generations than it was for them to know they were the descendants of a president of the United States.

Similarly, many descendants of Civil War soldiers, both Blacks and Whites, have no idea that one or more of their ancestors had served in that war. Through the years, families have scattered and lost touch with relatives who may have known. The majority of them, however, probably did not put much in writing except perhaps in family Bibles, including records of marriages, births, and deaths. Consequently, not much family history may have passed to the next generations.

In my own family, few living descendants of Crowder Patience knew about their Grandpa's Civil War service until my first book ***Created to Be Free*** was published in 2001. Because I had been reared in the same small borough where Grandpa is buried, I know much of the history of our family and I believe I have the responsibility to share it with others. I am pleased to know that several younger relatives have developed an interest in learning about their ancestors.

Regarding my original research, a newspaper article, "Putting Together Pieces of a Civil War Puzzle: Retired Teacher has Rewritten History," was written by Timothy Wilson. It was published in the *Washington Post* on 31 August 2008.[46]

Presently, many descendants are becoming aware of the forgotten Civil War soldiers in their families. For instance, in 2009 descendants of Pvt. Amos McKinney [47] were delighted to learn about their ancestor's service in the 1st Alabama Cavalry.[48] Three generations were present at a ceremony to honor their ancestor on 11 July 2009, ninety years after his burial in the Magnolia-Sykes Cemetery in Decatur, Alabama.

A newspaper article, "More Than 200 Gather to Honor Civil War Veteran. Soldier, ex-slave gets grave marker nearly 100 years after his death," was written by Deangelo McDaniel and published in *The Decatur Daily*.[49]

Re-enactors
13th U.S. Colored Troops
Living History Association
2009
(Photo courtesy of Reba N. Burruss-Barnes)

Also unaware of their illustrious ancestor until 2012 were descendants of the Medal of Honor Recipient Bruce Anderson. Due to the research of Montgomery County Historian Kelly Yacobucci Farquhar, Levi Pascher wrote a newspaper article, "A History of Service; Historian links local WWII veteran to Civil War hero." It was published in *The Leader Herald* in Gloversville, N.Y., on 11 November 2012. [50]

During the Civil War, Pvt. Bruce Anderson of the 142nd New York Infantry volunteered with twelve others to advance the palisade, an almost impossible undertaking. His first act of bravery, though, was substituting for a married soldier who had two small children. His second was being willing to walk into what could be certain death from which only he and one other would manage to escape. Not until fifty years later in 1914 would he receive the Medal of Honor because, so it was reported, his recommendation report had been misplaced.[51]

He, his first wife Adelia, and their children lived in Gloversville for a number of years, but following a divorce and a second marriage, Bruce Anderson moved to Amsterdam, N.Y. There he died in 1922 at the age of seventy-seven years.

According to the article, historian Kelly Farquhar had discovered a possible descendant of Bruce Anderson. He is World War II veteran Ambrose Anderson, Jr. who lives in a town close to Gloversville. In June 2012 he attended an award ceremony in Washington, D.C., for the Montford Point Marines when each received a bronze replica of the Congressional Gold Medal.

Kelly Farquhar wanted concrete evidence to prove that both the grandfather and the grandson had received the highest honor for their service to their country. The necessary proof was found in the *Gloversville Leader* in a 1936 obituary for Clara Bell Anderson Bowman. Included were the names of her half-siblings, the children of Bruce Anderson and his second wife. Further proof is found in the 1880 census which recorded seven year-old Clara Bell

Anderson as the sister of twelve year-old Ambrose Anderson, father of Ambrose "Cowboy" Anderson. [52]

Surprised by such news, Ambrose "Cowboy" Anderson realized that he also had proof of his relationship to Bruce Anderson. It is found in a collage of family photos shot at a gathering years ago. There he was at about 12 years-old, standing between his Aunt Clara and her husband Elmer. This example certainly demonstrates how important censuses, obituaries, and family photographs can be to descendants searching for ancestors.

Name:	**Bruce Anderson**
Side:	Union
Regiment State/Origin:	New York
Regiment Name:	142 N.Y. Infantry.
Regiment Name Expanded:	142nd Regiment, New York Infantry
Company:	K
Rank In:	Private
Rank In Expanded:	Private
Rank Out:	Private
Rank Out Expanded:	Private
Film Number:	M551 roll 3

Pvt. Bruce Anderson [53]
Ancestry.com

CHAPTER 5

RECRUITMENT OF BLACK SOLDIERS

War Department General Orders No. 143 was issued on 22 May 1863 to organize Black segregated regiments commanded solely by White officers. This is a fifth category of Black soldiers.

Almost immediately, the Governor of Massachusetts, John A. Andrew, began recruiting free Blacks. Flyers [54] were distributed near and far, from Massachusetts to Pennsylvania, Ohio, other northern states, and even to Canada.

Working to fill a first regiment of 1,000, recruiters included prominent Blacks such as Frederick Douglass and the former "patriot" William Henry Johnson. The 54th Massachusetts Volunteers was the first northern Black regiment to be organized and among the recruits were two of Frederick Douglass's sons, Louis and Charles. The white officers were handpicked by Governor Andrew himself.

Twenty-three-year-old Col. Robert Gould Shaw[55] was the chosen officer to lead this regiment which would have such great importance. First, because unlike the other Black regiments already organized in the South, it was comprised of freed Blacks, many educated, who resided in the northeast states.

Forming this Black regiment around the time of President Lincoln's Emancipation Proclamation in the midst of the Civil War gives a second aspect of its importance. Glimpsed in the 1989 movie *Glory*, was how the future of all Black regiments would rest on the conduct of the 54th Massachusetts in battle.

Sgt. William Carney
54th Massachusetts Infantry

And it did perform valiantly. In fact, the first Black Medal of Honor recipient served in that regiment. He was Sgt. William Carney[56] considered the first recipient, even though he would not receive his medal until 1900, thirty-seven years after his bravery at Ft. Wagner.

The first four northern Black regiments were raised in the states of Massachusetts and Connecticut and retained their state designations throughout the war: 54th and 55th Massachusetts.

Infantry, 5th Massachusetts Cavalry, and 29th Connecticut Infantry, comprising a fifth category.

With great confidence and high expectations on 28 May 1863, Col. Shaw's regiment proudly marched down Beacon Street, departing Boston for the South. A bronze 1894 Robert Gould Shaw and the Massachusetts 54th Regiment Memorial in Boston depicts the Colonel on horseback and three rows of proud infantry men marching behind.

Robert Gould Shaw Memorial[57]
Boston, Massachusetts
Augustus Saint-Gaudens, Sculptor
(from author's collection)

Next is the sixth category, the United States Colored Troops (U.S.C.T.), referred to by Frederick Douglass as Lincoln's "Sable Arm."[58] Eventually there would be 120 infantry regiments, twelve heavy regiments, ten light artillery batteries, and seven cavalry units. According to War Department records, the U.S.C.T. made up 10% of the Union Army and fought in 449 engagements on land and sea, including thirty-nine major battles.

What induced those Black men to enlist in the Union Army? Perhaps by what flyers offered. Incentives were being offered to men who heretofore only had impossible dreams!

BOUNTY $100!

AT THE EXPIRATION OF THE TERM OF SERVICE.

Pay, $13 a Month!

Good Food & Clothing!

State Aid to Families!

Medal of Honor winner Sgt. Major Christian Fleetwood of the 4th U.S.C.T. would share his reasons. ***"A double purpose induced me and most others to enlist--to assist in abolishing slavery and to save the country from ruin."*** [59]

CHAPTER 6

GENERAL ORDERS No. 323 AND THE UNDERCOOKS

A seventh category includes the Black soldiers like my great grandfather, who did not serve with the U.S.C.T. They were the Blacks who enlisted in the Union Army as undercooks according to:

GENERAL ORDERS No. 323 [60]

WAR DEPT., ADJT. GENERAL'S OFFICE,
Washington, September 28, 1863.

In section 10, act of March 3, 1863, it is enacted "That the President of the United States be, and he is hereby, authorized to cause to be enlisted for each cook (to allowed by section 9) two undercooks of African descent, who shall receive for their full compensation $10 per month and one ration per day; $3 of said monthly pay may be in clothing.

For a regular company, the two undercooks will be enlisted; for a volunteer company, they will be mustered into service, as in the cases of other soldiers. In each case a remark will be made on their enlistment papers showing that they are undercooks of African descent. Their names will be borne on the company muster-rolls at the foot of the list of privates. They will be paid, and their accounts will be kept, like other enlisted men. They will also be discharged in the same manner as other soldiers.

By order of the Secretary of War:

E. D. TOWNSEND,
Assistant Adjutant-General.

FORTY-NINTH INFANTRY. 507

Name and Rank.	Residence.	Date of rank or enlistment.	Date of muster.	Remarks.
Turner, Rosander	Wabash co	Jan. 1, 1862		Mustered out Jan. 9, 1865
Washburn, Edward	Centralia	Dec. 2, 1863	Jan. 31, 1864	Died at home, about Oct. 8, 1864
Weldon, Charles J	Salem	Jan. 18, 1862		Disch. Sept. 13, '62; disabil.
Wilson, John C	Decatur	Jan. 28, 1862	June 10, 1863	Abs't, sick at M.O. of Reg't.
White, Abner		Mar. 3, 1863	June 19, 1863	Mustered out Sept. 9, 1865.
Wincks, James	Alma	Nov. 30, 1863	Dec. 31, 1863	" "
Williamson, Vincent P	Salem	Dec. 24, 1863	Jan. 31, 1864	" "
Williams, Clement M.	"	Jan. 22, 1864	Feb. 22, 1864	M. O. Sept. 9, '65; wounded.
Winans, Joseph	New Liberty	Apr. 7, 1865	Apr. 7, 1865	Mustered out Sept. 9, 1865.
Under Cooks of A. D.				
Maybry, John		Nov. 25, 1863	Dec. 21, 1863	Mustered out Sept. 9, 1865.
Williams, George		Dec. 19, 1863	"	" "

***UnderCooks of A.D.*[61]**
<u>John Maybry and George Williams</u>
49th Illinois Co. D

What about women? Is Laura Wisdom [62] not a Black Civil War soldier, then, since she enlisted under General Orders 323? Here is a research project in the waiting. "The First Black Female Soldiers Served in the Civil War."

W | 49 | Ill.

Laura Wisdom

Under Cook Co. K, 49 Reg't Illinois Infantry.

Appears on

Company Muster Roll

for Sept & Oct, 1863.

Present or absent Present

Stoppage, $ 100 for

Due Gov't, $ 100 for

Remarks: Enlisted as Under Cook Genl Orders No 323 in accordance with section 10 Act March 3rd/63 (Enrolled June 29/63 at Germantown.)

only Roll on which name appears.

Book mark:

(868) Copyist.

<u>Laura Wisdom</u> [63]
<u>Under Cook</u> Co. K, 49th Reg't Illinois Infantry.
Appears on
Company Muster Roll
for <u>Sept. and Oct., 1863</u>
Present

*Remarks: **<u>Enlisted as UnderCook under Gen. Orders No 323 in accordance with section Act</u>** <u>March 3rd/63 at Germantown</u>*

Only roll on which name appears

CHAPTER 7

THREE UNDERCOOKS GARRISONED AT PLYMOUTH, NORTH CAROLINA

My serious research of Black Civil War soldiers began with the thirteen cooks serving in four of the nine regiments garrisoned at Plymouth, North Carolina, in 1864. Following the Yankee defeat at Plymouth, on the 20th of April, most of the Black cooks and the forty or so recruits who had been waiting for their orders had been either killed or remanded back into slavery which was in complete contradiction to the Union's demands that Black soldiers were to be treated as prisoners of war.

By intent, newspapers reported nothing concerning the fate of Blacks at Plymouth. Fearful of the Federal reaction to captured Black soldiers and sailors being returned to their masters rather than being treated as prisoners of war, President Jefferson Davis had directed North Carolina's Governor Zebulon Vance to make certain that such information would never reach the newspapers.[64]

Since the Confederates refused to comply with the Federals, Gen. Ulysses S. Grant, unfortunately coinciding with the date of the Battle of Plymouth, shut down the prisoner exchanges with the hope that it would cause the Confederates to change their minds. Because that did not happen, thousands of soldiers from both sides would suffer and perish at each side's deplorable military prisons.

The following historical marker in Plymouth, North Carolina, commemorates the nine Yankee regiments that were garrisoned there in April 1864, as well as the Black recruits waiting to join their regiments.

<u>Siege of Plymouth Historic Marker</u>
Plymouth, North Carolina
(from the author's collection)

"PLYMOUTH PILGRIMS"
16th Connecticut Volunteer Infantry
2nd Massachusetts Heavy Artillery - Companies G & H
12th New York Cavalry - Companies A & F
24th Independent Battery B New York Veteran Light Artillery
85th New York Veterans Volunteer Infantry
2nd North Carolina Union Volunteers - Companies B & E
3rd Pennsylvania Heavy Artillery - Detachment Co A
101st Pennsylvania Veteran Volunteer Infantry
103rd Pennsylvania Veteran Volunteer Infantry
10th U.S. Colored Infantry- Recruits
37th U.S. Colored Infantry - Recruits
2nd U.S. Colored Cavalry - Recruits
U.S. Army Gunboats Bombshell and Dolly
UNION NAVAL FORCES
U.S.S. Miami
U.S.S. Southfield
U.S.S. Massasoit
U.S.S. Whitehead
U.S.S. Ceres

Dedicated on the 135th Anniversary - April 17, 1999

The sign honors the Union forces, both Army and Navy, which fought valiantly at Plymouth, N.C. The defeated Yankees were dubbed "Plymouth Pilgrims" [65] because they were wearing their dress uniforms when forced to march into the infamous Andersonville Prison. Seems that the dress "Hardee" hats [66]worn by some of the Yankees reminded their captors of the Pilgrims of Plymouth, Massachusetts.

A provocative article was published in 1996 in the *North Carolina Journal* [67] in which this question was discussed, "Had there been a massacre of Black soldiers on the 20th of April 1864 at Plymouth following the battle?" Several eye witnesses, including Charlie Mosher, 85th N.Y. Infantry, stated there had been,[68] while others vehemently denied the allegations.

To this day these questions still remain unanswered, "What happened to the recruits of the 2nd U.S Colored Cavalry or of the 37th US. Colored Infantry whose regiments are listed on the historical marker? And what happened to each of the thirteen Black cooks?"

Some were accounted for, both those who died and those who survived. However, others were listed on their regimental rosters as "unaccounted for," translating into "presumed dead."

Definitely known, though, is what happened to Privates John Rolack (Rolak, Roulac), Richard West, and Crowder Pacien (Patient, Pacient, Patience) following the battle. Pvt. John Rolack, a Bertie County contraband cook in the 85th N.Y. garrisoned at Plymouth, was described on his military papers as hazel-eyed with light hair. A twenty-year-old Mulatto, but undetected as one, he was captured and sent to Andersonville where, unfortunately, he died six months later from the ravages of the Prison. [69]

Out of the approximately 45,000 Yankees who had been incarcerated at the Andersonville Prison, 776 were U.S.C.T. prisoners of war. [70] Pvt. John Rolack was not with that number.

Pvt. John Rolack's Grave
Andersonville Prison
(Courtesy of Don Pettijohn, Park Ranger)

Why were there so few Blacks at Andersonville Prison? Because it was unusual for captured Blacks to be sent to the prisons since they were valuable "property" needed to be returned to their masters. Or because any Black caught in uniform was to be tried as slave insurrectionists and sentenced to death. Or because many Blacks were killed under the black flag of "no quarter," meaning "no mercy," such as what happened at Ft. Pillow, Tennessee.[71]

Captured at Plymouth, but not killed because he had not been wearing his blue uniform, Pvt. Richard West Co. I of the 103rd Pennsylvania Volunteers was remanded back into slavery and put to work for the Confederates at Rainbow Bluff. Later, however, he managed to escape and returned to his regiment reconstituted on Roanoke Island.

His story is an illustration of the Confederates' refusal to treat captured Black soldiers as prisoners of war as the Union demanded. Instead, according to Confederate President Jefferson Davis, captured Blacks were to be sent back to their owners if known. If not, they were to be put to work for the Confederacy which is exactly what happened to Richard West, but it was not the end of his story. His deposition tells it all. [72]

DEPOSITION taken under general letter of instructions of December 18, 1900 relative to Norfolk, Va. cases.

Case of Richard West Inv. Ctf., No. 951181

On this 11 day of March, 1902, at Norfolk, county of Norfolk, State of Va., before me, G. D. F. Mc Sorley, a special examiner of the Bureau of Pensions, personally appeared Richard West, who, being by me first duly sworn to answer truly all interrogatories propounded to him during this special examination of aforesaid claim for pension, deposes and says:

Deposition …Case of Richard West Inv. Ctg, No 951181

DEPOSITION taken under general letter of instructions of December 18, 1900 relative to Norfolk, Va. Cases.

On this 11 day of March, 1902, at Norfolk, county of Norfolk, State of Va., before me, C. D. F. McSorley, a special examiner of the Bureau of Pensions, personally appeared Richard West, who, being by me first duly sworn to answer truly all interrogatories propounded to him during this special examination of aforesaid claim for pension, deposes and says:

I am about 59 years of age, occupation, am an employee in the U.S. Navy Yard, Portsmouth, Va., residence Berkley, Norfolk Co., Va. And my post-office address is the same.

I was born in Bertie Co., N.C. near Windsor. Was born a slave to Cannie West but he is dead. My father's name was Jerry West and my mother's name was Tildei West and both of them belonged to my master. My full and correct name is Richard West and I have never been known under any other name. I got my name from my father and mother.

I was about 21 years of age when I enlisted as a Private in Co I 103rd Pa., V. I. in March, but I can't give you the year. I enlisted at Plymouth, N.C. Was examined at enlistment but not stripped and was sworn in at Plymouth. I can't recollect the name of the recruiting officer.

I was discharged at New Berne, N.C. in June, but can't give the year. I think I must have served about a year and a half.

I have my original discharge certificate which I now show you. (Exhibited and shown that Richard West a Colored undercook of 1st Lt. William H. Kiester's Company (I) 103rd PA. Inf. Vet. Vols. Was enrolled on the First of March 1864 and discharged 25th of June 1865 at New Berne, N.C. Said Richard West was born in Bertie Co., N.C. is 21 years of age 5 ft. 7 in. high, dark complexion, dark eyes, dark hair and by occupation when enrolled a slave.)

Pensioner is now 5 ft. 5 in. tall, black complexion, hair and eyes, hair mixed with gray. I was shot in the left leg at Plymouth, N.C. in the calf of the leg and that is the only mark or scar I have on my person. Says he has grown down since discharge.

Immediately after my muster out at New Bern I went up to Pa. to Butler Co. and was discharged there and paid off. Then I came here to Norfolk and have resided in this vicinity ever since.

I have never rendered any other service, military or naval, Union or Confederate.

After I enlisted I was made Company Cook and served in that capacity until I was captured by the Confederate forces at Plymouth about a year after my enlistment. The southern troops made me work on the breast works then at Rainbow Bluff up beyond Plymouth on the Roanoke River for nine months and eight days and then on a Sunday morning bare headed and bare footed I made my escape and joined the Yankees at Plymouth. It took me five days to get down to Plymouth.

My feet were so frost bitten when I got to Plymouth that I was placed aboard the hospital ship a double ender flag ship, name unknown and after I was on her two months I was sent down to New Bern. My company had been captured the same time I was and I had not seen them up to this time. I was taken to headquarters at New Bern and got some new clothes and then I was sent back to Roanoke Island under Captain Coffey of Co. C of my regiment and remained there until I was discharged.

at Roanoke Island?
J. H. Gorth
Richard his X mark West
Deponent.

Sworn to and subscribed before me this 11 day of March 190?, and I certify that the contents were fully made known to deponent before signing.

Special Examiner.

Richard West's pension application and the War Department's authorization both contained information concerning the fate of one of the Blacks at Plymouth following the Yankee defeat. Except for Pvt. John Roulac, they did not become prisoners of war as were the white "Plymouth Pilgrims" and sent to Andersonville Prison.

No. 759.957

WAR DEPARTMENT,
RECORD AND PENSION DIVISION.

Washington, D. C., APR 16 1890, 18

Respectfully returned to the Commissioner of Pensions.

Richard West (Col'd.)
Co. I 103 Reg't Pa. Vols
was enrolled March 1, 1864
and mustered out June 25, 1865

He was captured at Plymouth N.C. Apl 20/64.

From Mch 1, 1864, to June 25, 1865
he held the rank of Colored Under Cook

and during that period the rolls show him present except as follows:

Apl 30/65 (Prior borne) Captured at Plymouth N.C. Apl 20/64. Subsequently escaped, should have been mustered [illegible] on former rolls instead of Geo. C. Freeman.

Write nothing to the left of this line.

Richard West (Col'd)
103rd Pennsylvania Volunteers Co. I

No. <u>759.957</u>

WAR DEPARTMENT

RECORD AND PENSION DIVISION

Washington, D.C. <u>April 16, 1890</u>

Respectfully returned to the Commissioner of Pensions.

<u>Richard West (Cold.) Co I 103 Reg't Pa. Vols.</u>

was enrolled <u>March 1, 1864</u> and <u>mustered out June 25, 1865</u>

<u>He was captured at Plymouth, N.C. Apr. 20/64.</u>

From <u>March 1, 1864</u> to June 25, 1865 he held the rank of <u>Colored Under Cook.</u>

and during that period the rolls show him present except as follows:

<u>April 30/65 (first ???)</u>

<u>Captured at Plymouth, N.C. April 20/64, subsequently</u>

<u>escaped, should have been mustered present on former rolls instead of Geo. E. Freeman.</u>

<u>Prisoners of War Records furnished no information . Other</u>

<u>records furnish nothing additional bearing upon the case.</u>

Another Black serving as a cook for the Yankees at Plymouth, N.C., prior to the April 1864 battle was my great-grandfather, Crowder Patience. A seventeen year-old runaway slave, a "contraband," he had enlisted in the 103rd Pennsylvania Volunteers.

<u>Crowder Patience at Age 81</u>
Standing soldier-straight in front of his Pennsylvania home ca. 1928 (Author's collection)

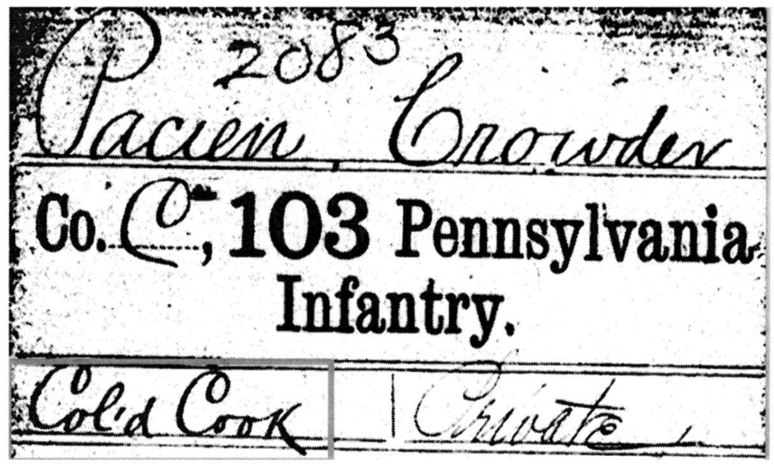

2083

Pacien Crowder

Co. C, 103 Pennsylvania Infantry.

Col'd Cook | Private

When researching the military records of Black cooks, one will find different racial identifications such as "Col'd cook," "cook," "contraband," "A. D" (African Descent), "servant," "negro," but never "Black." That word was reserved for blacksmiths and not as a racial identity.

The Roster of the 103rd Pennsylvania Volunteers [74] states that Crowder Pacien "apparently escaped capture following the battle on April 20, 1864." Of course, I wanted to know how that had been possible when all of the Yankees were either killed or sent to Andersonville.

The answer is due to fate or luck, as some might say. My ancestor was not at Plymouth when the battle erupted. Rather, he was on Roanoke Island with his company.[75] Each of the nine regiments garrisoned at Plymouth would rotate one of its companies for six months at a time to Roanoke Island to guard the Atlantic coast. Company C had just been rotated with Company F in January, the former sailing to safety, and the latter, unfortunately, to defeat and Andersonville Prison in Georgia.

Sunday Independent, May 20, 1928 [76]
Wilkes-Barre, Penna.

CIVIL WAR VETERAN OF UNUSUAL CAREER IS VALLEY RESIDENT

Crowder Pacient Lived In Slavery Before The Emancipation Proclamation Of President Lincoln And When Opportunity Permitted He Joined Forces With His Deliverer.

KEEN IN RECOLLECTIONS

Few days of the year carry more meaning with them than Memorial Day. Once in each twelve months it is observed and throughout the land the disappearing ranks of the Blue and Gray form in line for the parade of honor to their departed comrades. Sixty-three years have passed since the last shots of the great Civil War were fired and few of the heroes remain.

As the lines are formed this year and the veterans grouped in the cars which will carry them along the line of march, to no one present will such a stream of memories return as to one wearer of the Blue from Exeter. To no other man in Wyoming Valley has such a great wealth and variety of experiences been vouchsafed.

An old and respected colored man is the one in mind. Now eighty-two years of age, a slave in the South before the war, a soldier in the Union Army, a farmer of old Wyoming Valley and a man who has held only two positions--both of trust--for the past sixty years, who else could hold such a position in life here? Crowder Pacient is the name of this respected resident.

Crowder Pacient lives now with his wife and daughter on Susquehanna [77]Avenue, Exeter, just across the road from the golf course of the Fox Hill Country Club on the road which cuts from Exeter to the Susquehanna Trail above West Pittston.

There he lives in a house provided after the smaller place in which he had spent many years had outlived its usefulness. From there he has sent the rest of his family--four boys and a girl [78] *out into the world.*

Up until two years ago Pacient worked steadily for the Carpenter family, one of the original settlers of that part of the Valley. He came to the family, to the partnership of Jesse and Isaac Carpenter, in the Fall of 1883. Work with horses is connected with his entire life. Two years ago, after going back to work too soon after a siege of pneumonia his need of a rest became apparent, his team of horses was shot and he, in his forty-fifth year with the Carpenter family is an honored retainer whose loyal services are respected.

Enlisted in War

When the great war between the North and the South first broke out, Crowder Pacient was one of the thousands of young Negro slaves in South [79] *Carolina. With the coming of the war to free him and his race, naturally his sympathies turned to that cause which was for his betterment. At first too young to take active part, there finally came his chance. On April 4, 1864, at the age of eighteen, he took advantage of the opportunity offered and enlisted with the 103rd Infantry from Pennsylvania, then in South* [80] *Carolina. He joined Company C of that regiment, most of which was enlisted in the western part of the state and in the Pittsburgh district.*

He was with this outfit through the rest of the war and came North with it. The last pay was given the men at Harrisburg and here Pacient left the 103rd. He was honorably discharged on June 25, 1865. Shortly afterward he located in Mechanicsville [Mechanicsburg] *and remained there about a year. "Long enough to be married," he says.*

It was here that the horse began to become the force which directed his life activities. From his memory which is most remarkably keen, he recalls that a man named Green was shipping some horses to Pittston and he went with them. After delivering the horses he stayed in this section, first becoming employed on a farm along the Sullivan Trail.

Work on the farm was scarse in the Winter and he turned to find other employment. His skill with horses again stood him in good stead and he was taken on by J. B. Schooley, a member of another pioneer family. With the Schooley retinue he was a coachman and he remained with that family for seventeen years until 1883.

Then forty-five years ago, he was put in charge of the horses of Jesse Carpenter and his association with that family still exists. It is such an example of loyalty on the part of the toiler and appreciation by the employer that would be most difficult to duplicate. It is fine and inspiring.

The Day of Big Farms

As is to be expected, most of Crowder Pacient's work with the Carpenters was with horses. For many years he was a teamster. Back in those days the farm on which he worked extended from the mountain to the river--as did all the old farms--and even included the island in the Susquehanna. That was also worked, says Pacient, and he remembers when a good crew of fifteen hoemen were needed there.

His memory needs no special effort to bring back the past and he tells of the long drives with the horses, necessary trips then: the regular drives to Wilkes-Barre, Scranton, and beyond; back of the mountain, too. "And at times," he says, "I'd be so tired I could just drop down back of the horses and sleep."

But now Crowder Pacient's work with horses is over. He has seen the auto and the tractor slowly crowd them off the roads and fields and now his last team has been shot, so that his labors might end. But Pacient keeps busy. A neat lawn about his home and his tidy little garden show the results of his work. The only effect of his illness is "a bit of stiffness in my knee and leg," he says. He is really a remarkably well preserved and able man for his years.

He has kept up his active membership in the G.A.R., attends the meetings whenever able to do so, meets his old comrades of the war regularly and hopes to be able to take part in the Memorial Day parade this year. He wasn't sure he could but he was going to try hard. His place would be hard to fill and he will be sorely missed if not there.

The natural romance and interest which surrounds this old man from the South produce many legends concerning him, through the section in which he lives. The most popular is that Jesse Carpenter found him on the battlefield. It claims he ran up to Carpenter in the midst of battle, seeking assistance and remained with him to be brought home.

Crowder Pacient went into the Union Army of his own accord and was honorably discharged. Then following the trail of the hoof print, he came into Wyoming Valley and he still is here. Always with horses, he remained at his post until his last team was shot and laid to rest so that he, too, might also have peace and quiet.

<u>Crowder Patience With G.A.R.[81] Comrades</u>
Wyoming Valley, Penna.
2nd Row , 2nd from right
(Courtesy of Marian Patience Henry)

OBITUARY

Pittston Gazette February 4, 1930

Crowder Patience Buried With Full Military Honor.

Three veterans of the Civil War and a detail of Spanish-American war veterans were in attendance at the home and at the grave. The casket was draped with the American flag.

At the West Pittston Cemetery where the burial was made, a detail of Spanish-American War veterans fired a volley over the grave and taps were sounded.

Pvt. Crowder Patience
103rd Pennsylvania Volunteers
West Pittston Cemetery
(from author's collection)

NAME OF SOLDIER:	Pacien, Crowder (alias)			
	Patient, Crowder			
NAME OF DEPENDENT:	Widow Patient, Elsie Veden Minor			
SERVICE:	C 103 Pa Inf			
DATE OF FILING:	CLASS	APPLICATION NO.	CERTIFICATE NO.	STATE FROM WHICH FILED
1891 Nov 30	Invalid,	1074.766	1140.513	Pa
1930 Feb 13	Widow,	1,661,087	A 4 – 14-'30'	Pa
	Minor,			
ATTORNEY:	R. E. Bennett			

Elsie Patience's Civil War Widow's Application for Pension
(Author's Collection - -facsimile)

Two different ways of spelling the family's surname are apparent on this widow's pension application. As had the widow of Pvt. Ephraim Pierce, Elsie Vedan Patience would have had to submit affidavits to prove her claim as the widow of Pvt. Crowder Patience.

I have written to the Department of Veterans Affairs several times for copies of the original applications for both the veteran and his widow, but to no avail. This is an example of how arduous and sometimes disappointing this kind of research can be. On the other hand, it can be most rewarding.

CHAPTER 8

A TRIP TO THE CARLISLE BARRACKS

With the names I had discovered at Plymouth, I knew then of thirteen Black soldiers who had served in white regiments. Would that be enough to prove my hypothesis that there had been more than one Black soldier serving in one white regiment? So realizing that I needed the advice of an expert in Civil War history, I met with the Chairman of the History Department at Wilkes University in Wilkes-Barre, Pennsylvania, where I had earned my Bachelor's degree. I asked Dr. Harold Cox if he had ever heard of Black soldiers serving in white Civil War regiments.

"Never," he answered. Since he was so intrigued by my great grandfather's story, he encouraged me to continue researching for more such soldiers, suggesting that if I could find the names of at least 100 Black soldiers in white regiments, I would have proven my hypothesis.

His suggestion was that I should make a trip to the Carlisle Barracks [83] near Harrisburg, Pennsylvania, to see what information I could find there about Black soldiers who had served in Pennsylvania white regiments. After entering the research center, I approached Dr. Charles Summers, a staff member, to explain why I was there and with the expectation to experience the same surprise look I had gotten from others when I said I was looking for the names of Blacks who had served in white regiments

To my surprise, however, Dr. Summers seemed not to be surprised at all. He just said, "Please wait here a moment."

Returning a few minutes later, he was carrying a manila folder containing the military records of Pvt. Charles Graffell who had served as a cook in the 2nd California Cavalry Co. H. Seems that someone had inquired about this man way back in 1948.

1 | 2 Cav. | Cal.

Charles Graffel

Appears with rank of Private on

Muster and Descriptive Roll of a Detachment of U. S. Vols. forwarded.

for the 2d Reg't California Cav. Roll dated

Sacramento Cal, Jan 3, 1865.

Where born Cincinnati Ohio

Age 18 y'rs; occupation Cook

When enlisted Jan 3, 1865.

Where enlisted Sacramento

For what period enlisted 3 years.

Eyes Black; hair Black

Complexion Dark; height 5 ft. 7 in.

When mustered in Jan 3, 1865.

Where mustered-in Sacramento

Bounty paid $ 100; due $ 100

Where credited

Company to which assigned H

Valuation of horse, $ 100

Valuation of horse equipments, $ 100

Remarks: Credited to the 1st Sub Dist Sacramento Co. Middleport Cal Colored under cook

Book mark:

D P Webster

(339) Copyist.

Muster Roll for Pvt. Charles Graffell [84]
2nd California Cavalry

SOUTHERN DIVISION.

Department of the Interior,

BUREAU OF PENSIONS,

Charles S. Graffell
Co. K, 2 Reg't Calif. V. Cav.

Washington, D. C., March 6, 1911

SIR: To aid this Bureau in preventing anyone falsely personating you, or otherwise committing fraud in your name, or on account of your service, you are required to answer fully the questions enumerated below.

You will please return this circular under cover of the inclosed envelope which requires no postage.

Very respectfully,

Mr. Charles S. Graffell
Goldfield
Nevada

J. L. Davenport
Commissioner.

1. Where were you born? Answer. Cincinnatia Ohio
2. Where did you enlist? Answer. Sacramento California
3. Where had you lived before you enlisted? Answer. Marysville yuba co.
4. What was your occupation? Answer. Left home and inlisted. worked at blacksmith trade
5. Were you a slave? If so, state the names of all former owners, and particularly the name of your owner at the date of your enlistment. No never was slave
6. Where were you discharged? Answer. Camp Drum 18 miles from Los angeles
7. Where have you lived since discharge? Give dates, as nearly as possible, of any change of residence. Went to sanfrancisco marysville Tehama Redbluff Tehama County Calif. Went to Tehama Tehama in 1871 and ... lived ...
8. What is your present occupation? Answer. have followed ...
9. What is your height? 5 feet, 11 inches. The color of your skin? dark ...
Are there any permanent marks or scars on your person? If so, describe them. one stomach caused by horse falling on me when ... for service
10. Were you in the military or naval service under a name different from that by which you are now known? If so, state what it was. military Charles S. Graffell
11. Have you ever been known by any names other than that given in your application for pension? If so, state them in full. mother married twice was raised up under step father name chas. McGowan
12. By what name are you now known? State in full. Charles S. Graffell
13. What is your actual residence at the present time, and what is the nearest post-office? Answer. city of Goldfield state of Nevada

PENSION OFFICE APR 24 1911 U. S.

WITNESSES: 1. C. J. Hosman
2. R. W. Fields

(Witnesses who can write sign here.)

Date: March 13th, 1911

Department of the Interior [85]
Bureau of Pensions
Washington, D.C., March 6, 1911
Charles S. Graffell

DEPARTMENT OF THE INTERIOR
BUREAU OF PENSIONS
Washington, D.C., March 6, 1911

Sir: To aid this Bureau in preventing anyone falsely personating you, or otherwise committing fraud in your name, or on account of your service, you are required to answer fully the questions enumerated below,

You will please return this circular under cover of the inclosed envelie which requires no postage.

Very respectfully,

J.L.Davenport,
Commissioner

Mr. Charles S. Graffell
Goldfield
Nevada

1. ***Where were you born? Answer. Cincinnati, Ohio.***
2. ***Where did you enlist? Answer. Sacramento, California.***
3. ***Where had you lived before you enlisted? Answer. Maryville Yuba, Ca.***
4. ***What was your occupation? Answer. Worked at blacksmith trade, left home and inlisted.***
5. ***Were you a slave? If so, state the names of all former owners, and particularly the name of your owner at the date of your enlistment. No. Never was a slave.***
6. ***Where were you discharged? Answer. Camp Drumm 18 miles from Los Angeles***
7. ***Where have you lived since discharge? Give dates, as nearly as possible, on any changes of residence. Went to San Francisco, Maryville, Tehama, Redbluff, Tehama County, Calif.***
8. ***What is your present occupation? Answer. Have followed horseshoing all of my life.***
9. ***What is your height? 5 feet, 11 inches. The color of your skin? Dark.***

Are there any permanent marks or scars on your person? If so, describe them. <u>One on stomach caused by horse falling on me when braking for service.</u>

10. ***Were you in the military or naval service under a name different from that by which you are now known? If so, state what it was. <u>Military Charles S. Graffell</u>***
11. ***Have you ever been known by any name other than that given in your application for pension? If so, state them in full. <u>Mother married twice, was raised up under stepfather's name Chas. Mc Gowan.</u>***
12. ***By what name are you now known? State in full. <u>Charles S. Graffell</u>***
13. ***What is your actual residence at the present time, and what is the nearest post-office? Answer. <u>City of Goldfield State of Nevada</u>***

Date- March 13th, 1911

OCTOGENARIAN [86]

Military Funeral for Charles Graffell
February 20, 1931

With the Rev. C. M. Julian, Minister of the Red Bluff Methodist Church officiating, impressive military funeral services were held yesterday for Charles Graffell, 80, Civil War veteran, for 74 years a resident of California, who died at his home late Friday night.

Burial was at Oak Hill Cemetery where a firing squad in command of Col. E. A. Lewis and composed of Sam Reed, Max Holiday, Charles W. Pramme, W. H. Ludwig, and Henry J. Schafer, members of the Spanish War veterans, fired a salute over the grave. Taps were sounded by Douglas Thorpe.

WAR DEPARTMENT
O. Q. M. G. Form No. 623
Approved Aug. 12, 1913
Revised July 11, 1929

ORIGINAL

APPLICATION FOR HEADSTONE

(PLEASE MAKE OUT AND RETURN IN DUPLICATE)

Name	Rank	Company	U. S. Regiment, State Organization, or Vessel	Date of Death
Charles Graffell	Cook	H	2nd Regiment California Cavalry	Feb. 20, 19

Name of Cemetery	Located in or near— City	State	If World War Veteran— Division	State	Hebrew Cross
Oak Hill Cemetery	Red Bluff	Calif.	*******		

TO BE SHIPPED TO James Montandon (Name of consignee) Red Bluff, California (Give town, county, and State)

POST OFFICE ADDRESS OF CONSIGNEE Red Bluff, Calif.

MAR 5 1931

DO NOT WRITE HERE

Verified

Ordered LEE MASS. APR 8 1931

From

Shipped 4-28-31

I hereby agree to accept the headstone at above destination, freight prepaid, and properly place same at decedent's grave.

This application is for the UNMARKED grave of Charles Graffell. It is understood the stone will be furnished and delivered at the railroad station or steamboat landing above indicated, at Government expense, freight prepaid, and agreed it will be promptly removed and set up at private expense.

252200

Mrs Hattie Graffell Applicant.

Address Red Bluff Calif Date Feb. 25 1931

Pvt. Charles Graffell [87]
Union HeadstoneApplication
2nd California Cavalry Co. H

Quite flabbergasted, I asked Dr. Summers how he could remember the name of Charles Graffell from fifty-one years before. Why, after all, this was 1999. He answered that at the time he had been so surprised by the information that it had just stuck with him.

Dr. Summers had no additional names to offer, though, suggesting that I try a book written by Samuel Bates. His book, ***The History of Pennsylvania Regiments*** contained roster lists from which I was able to discover the names of approximately 100 additional Black men who had served as cooks in Pennsylvania regiments. I found them listed at the base of the rosters where they followed the names of the recruits.

I wondered about that at the time. Why were their names listed after the names of the white soldiers? I just chalked it up to another way of discriminating, not knowing at that time about General Orders No. 323, but learning later from Bennie McCrae.[88]

That order was issued in 1863 after President Abraham Lincoln finally had signed the Emancipation Proclamation on 1 January 1863 and after General Orders No. 143 was issued to allow Blacks to become bona fide soldiers in the Union Army. By that time too many deaths had occurred due to disease and disastrous battles, as well as many desertions and a failed draft. An epiphany, perhaps, had come to the President that with Blacks serving in the ranks, he just might become victorious.

After all, was that not what Frederick Douglass had been pushing? Were Blacks not ready and willing, even his two sons, Charles and Louis? Was the Union Army not already using Blacks as laborers, teamsters, cooks, laundry workers, and anything else the white soldiers did not want to be? Douglass was proclaiming, "The president should use his 'Sable Arm.'"

Once the President finally allowed the formation of the segregated regiments, Blacks enlisted in droves as combatants. The 54th Massachusetts Infantry was the first to fill, quickly creating a need for a second regiment, the 55th Massachusetts Infantry. Besides Massachusetts residents enlisting, men travelled from other states near and far. They even came from Canada.

One such enthusiastic young soldier was Samuel James Patterson, my stepmother's grandfather. A free man, Pennsylvanian born and bred, he left home to join the 5th Massachusetts Cavalry.

However, in the white regiments, especially as they began to penetrate the South, readily available Blacks relieved the white soldiers from such menial jobs as cooks. After all, white men had not signed up to become cooks, but Black men expressly had. According to General Orders No. 323, they were to be ranked as soldiers and my great grandfather was among that number.

At the War College Barracks in 1998 I was able to collect 100 names to share with Dr. Harold Cox at Wilkes University and, as he had promised, he published an article about my research in the University newsletter. Furthermore, he encouraged me to continue researching because in the many years since the end of the Civil War, I seemed to be the only person interested in the topic of the Black soldiers who had served in white regiments.

I was asked during my C-Span presentation just how I went about finding additional names. My first batch were cooks like my ancestor who are racially identified in Broadfoot's *Roster of Union Civil War Soldiers 1861-1865*[89] and on their military records at the National Archives.

For my first publication I had simply intended to find 1,000 names to represent a full regiment, which I did with just thirteen of the states loyal to the Union. Then I "rested on my laurels," so to speak, until the time came when my publisher, Craig R. Scott, requested that I revise my small tome and complete all Union states.

Not only did I do that, I also learned from Glenda McWhirter Todd,[90] historian of the 1st Alabama Cavalry, that every Confederate state except South Carolina, had raised at least one

Union regiment. Until that revelation I had not thought to look in Confederate states for Black Union soldiers.

My publisher also wanted me to discover if Blacks had served in any other positions in white regiments besides as cooks. Those who had enlisted under General Orders No. 323; I had found easily. How, though, would I go about finding any other occupations? Broadfoot lists some, but not in great numbers.

Not until I received an e-mail just this past month from a fellow Civil War "buff," Goeffry Sattler, did I discover that *Ancestry.com* would provide me with hundreds of names of cooks and undercooks in all of the regiments. So much technology has changed since I began my "needle in a haystack" research sixteen years ago. No longer needed now is the Metro ride to the Archives during rush-hour to pore through books to find Blacks who served in white regiments. They are just a click away. Just have to place "undercook," and/or "Colored cook" in the "keyword" spot.

U.S. Civil War Soldiers, 1861-1865

Search

First & Middle Name(s) Last Name

Military

Year Location

Keyword

e.g. pilot or "Flying Tigers"

Search Clear Form

Soldier Search [91]
Ancestry.com

While I was still being amazed by the number of undercooks who I knew were Black from General Orders 323, I wondered what I could retrieve should I use “Colored teamster” as the keywords. When I did, names galore appeared. Then I tried “Colored blacksmith,” “Colored farrier,” and “Colored saddler.” Many of them had been in Cavalry regiments. **Note to researchers**: These are singular words. Do not add an “s.”

Because I have found so many names, too many to insert into this book, I have listed only enough A’s, B’s, and C’s for readers to become aware of the large number of forgotten Black soldiers. I cannot even imagine what the number might be, even should I research the entire alphabet.

Someone’s family lore may be that their Grandpa had served in the Civil War. His name is not on the Wall of Honor surrounding “The Spirit of Freedom” in Washington, D.C. Neither is it listed in my first volume of forgotten Black soldiers who served in white regiments. Perhaps, then, it might be found among the number left to discover on *Ancestry.com.*

Confusing to a researcher is the fact that listed in the above categories are many with only first names such as Abe who served in the 4th Iowa Cavalry Co. K or Eleck in the 92nd Illinois Infantry Co. H. [92] Such was the case of many contrabands who had absconded from slavery to join the Union Army. To discover who they became following the war would be a daunting endeavor, but with modern technology, perhaps not an impossible one for determined descendants.

CHAPTER 9

FINDING GRAVESITES OF BLACK SOLDIERS

Glenda McWhirter Todd, historian of the 1st Alabama Cavalry, discovered sixteen Black cooks in that regiment. She wondered if anyone else had done any research on Black soldiers who had served in white regiments and discovered that I had. She telephoned to ask if I would like to have copies of the military records she had collected. Her information arrived just in time to be published in my first revised edition in 2008.

During the next telephone call from Glenda, she informed me that she had located the burial site of one of the Blacks in the 1st Alabama Cavalry. He was Pvt. Simon West who had been buried in 1927 in an unmarked grave in Ohio. [93]

GRAVES REGISTRATION CARD — Cuyahoga Co.

Name: West, Samuel (Simon)
Address: 2906 Cedar Ave. Cleveland, Ohio
Date of Death: 1-25-1927 Place: Cleveland, Ohio
Cause: Pneumonia Date of Burial: 1-27-1927
Date of Birth: 3-5-1837 Place: Georgia
Name of Cemetery: Highland Park Loc.: Warrensville, Ohio
Govt. Tier 2
Lot No. 2 Section No. 3 Block No. - Grave No. 16
Marker: Flat - Upright - None X
Next of Kin: Katey West (Name) 2906 Cedar Ave. (Address)

SERVICE RECORD — Cemetery records indicate service.

War Served In: -
Date Enlisted - Date Discharged - Serial No. -
Branch of Service - Rank -
Company, Outfit or Ship

Glenda was instrumental in having a Union tombstone placed on the unmarked grave of Pvt. Simon West, a teamster in the 1st Alabama Cavalry. Moreover, she contacted Sandi Craighead who coordinated a memorial service participation of a local Boy

Scout troop and Civil War re-enactors to participate in a memorial service in the Highland Park Cemetery, Warrenville, Ohio. [94]

Pvt. Simon West
1st Alabama Cavalry
(Courtesy of Sandi Craighead and Glenda McWhirter Todd)

Then several months after the Simon West tombstone dedication in Ohio, Glenda McWhirter Todd telephoned to tell me that in the Magnolia-Sykes Cemetery located in Decatur, Alabama, she had discovered the gravesite of another 1st Alabama Black soldier.

Just how had she found Pvt. Amos McKinney? It happened this way. Peggy Allen Towns, [95] a Congressional aide for the 5th Congressional District and Rev. Wylheme Ragland were preparing to index the historic Black cemetery when they learned that Amos McKinney, a Civil War veteran, was buried there, but no one knew where. Luckily, his wife Lucinda's headstone is inscribed with "McKinney," and so that is how her husband's grave was located.

After the story about the indexing appeared in newspapers, Glenda Todd, telephoned Peggy Towns, Congressional aide to The Honorable Parker Griffith. Glenda then contacted the United States Department of Veterans Affairs to order a new marker for Pvt.

Amos McKinney, just as she had done for Pvt. Simon West the year before.

I was elated to be invited to participate in the ceremony.

You are cordially invited to attend the Memorial Dedication Ceremony for

Private Amos McKinney
United States Army
Company C, 1st Alabama Cavalry Regiment
Mustered In: Rome, Georgia on 15 December 1863
Mustered Out: Huntsville, Alabama on 20 October 1865
(Colored Union Civil War Soldier)

July 11, 2009 at 1:00 p.m.
Sykes Cemetery
Old Moulton Road, Decatur, Alabama

Reception following
King's Memorial United Methodist Church•702 McCartney Street NW, Decatur, Alabama 35601

For more information contact: Peggy Allen Towns (256) 345 9098
Wylheme Ragland (256) 353 9267

My publicist Reba N. Burruss-Barnes and I flew to Huntsville, Alabama, where we met Mrs. Johnnie McKinney Lester, the only living grandchild of Pvt. Amos McKinney. Having left Alabama many years ago for Chicago, when she had moved back to her home area she never expected to become the center of a fascinating bit of Civil War history. Her Grandpa's military service was to be recognized after all of these years. Even though she had an inkling about it, the subject was not discussed in her family. A Black having served in the Union Army was not something to brag about in Alabama.

Finally, after lying for ninety-nine years in an unmarked grave, Pvt. Amos McKinney is no longer one of the forgotten.

<u>***Pvt. Amos McKinney***</u>
1st Alabama Cavalry
(Photo courtesy of
Reba N. Burruss-Barnes)

<u>***Re-enactors Paying Homage***</u>
to the Memory of
Pvt. Amos McKinney
11 July 2009

Congressional Record

PROCEEDINGS AND DEBATES OF THE *111th* CONGRESS, FIRST SESSION

House of Representatives

TRIBUTE TO PRIVATE AMOS McKINNEY

HON. PARKER GRIFFITH, M.D. OF ALABAMA
July 11, 2009

MR. GRIFFITH. Madame Speaker, I rise today to recognize Private Amos McKinney. Private McKinney was a Black Soldier who served the United States Army in a White Regiment during the Civil War.

Amos McKinney started his service to our country at Rome, Georgia on December 15th, 1863 as an Undercook in Company C of the 1st Alabama Calvary. Enlisting as a cook was the avenue to combat for many African American soldiers during the Civil War, and Private McKinney was no different. During his service, he was shot below the knee and also suffered several wounds to his chest before being mustered out of service as a teamster, on October 20, 1865 in Huntsville, Alabama.

Unfortunately, history has forgotten many Black Soldiers who served the Union White Regiments during the Civil War. Driven by a firm belief in the Union's purpose, Private McKinney and others were willing to work their way up the ranks so they could fight for the cause. Their perseverance and courage should not be lost. In recognition of Private McKinney's service, there will be a dedication ceremony on July 11, 2009 for a memorial established in his honor.

Amos McKinney married Melissa Ann McAfee Pearson after the war, and together they had nine children. Private McKinney's courage is surely an inspiration to the family he left behind, and his bravery is a testament to the power of an unyielding American spirit and personal resolve.

Madame Speaker, I stand to recognize an American soldier and to extend my gratitude for the service of Private Amos McKinney and those who served beside him. I commend the McKinney family and the historians of my district whose efforts made this recognition possible.

Pvt. Amos McKinney Tribute
(Courtesy of Peggy Towns)

Many soldiers killed in battle were buried in mass graves. Others were carried home to be buried among family and friends. Ethel Washington, a New Jersey historian, has written a book citing hundreds of names of Black Civil War veterans who were buried in Union County, New Jersey.[96] In many areas of this country public cemeteries had Colored sections and many private cemeteries were located on church properties.

The original Civil War headstones consist of raised letters inside of a recessed shield. Many have disintegrated due to weathering through the years, considering that many are over 150 years-old. Many have been replaced by the Veterans Affairs or by families or others. Some never had a Union marker at all such as Private Debrix Miller of the 4th Michigan Infantry Co. F. Now 106 years after his death one sits on his grave.

<u>Pvt. Debrix Miller</u>
4th Michigan Infantry Co. F
(Courtesy of John C. Carter
Photo by Stephen P. Trammell)

John C. Carter, a member of the SUVCW (Sons of Union Veterans of the Civil War), S&DUSCT (Sons & Daughters of U.S. Colored Troops), and SCTLHA (U.S. Colored Troops Living History Association) provided the next name. In 2009 he applied for and was granted an approval for having an official Civil War headstone installed in Pittsford, Michigan, for Pvt. Debrix (Debary, Debris, Debra ire) who was listed as a "colored cook" or "cook of A.D." for Co. F of the 4th Michigan Infantry (re-organized.)

Found next to his wife's grave in the Pittsford Cemetery, the soldier's grave had been marked only with a small stone with the word "Father." It now is positioned in front of the brand new headstone.

A similar occurrence was published in an article by Dan Yount in *The Cincinnati Herald* on 31 October 2013, "Black, White Masons mark Black Civil War vets' graves." [97] He writes about the six unmarked graves of U.S.C.T. members who are buried in the Wesleyan Cemetery. The article discusses how the Veterans Administration recently changed policies concerning who can request Civil War tombstones. Seems that now only relatives may apply.

Unfortunately, direct relatives could be found for only two of the Black soldiers. So only they would receive tombstones from the Veterans Administration. Subsequently, both Black and White Cincinnati Masons joined to rectify the situation. Privates Taylor Bowen, Henry (Hanry) Clay, Richard B. Gordon, two different George Washingtons, John Yates, and U.S. Navy Seaman Daniel Harris Robinson now have Union headstones. [98] The owner of The Schott Monument Co., Jack Loos, donated four stones so all six could be honored at the same time.

A former Cincinnati Park Board naturalist, Kathy Dahl,[99] had worked on the tombstone project for two years and during one of her tours in the Wesleyan Cemetery she had pointed out the unmarked U.S.C.T. graves. From thence the project began.

Sgt. Barclay Stagner's information is provided by Nadia Orton, historian/genealogist. He served with the 8th Pennsylvania Volunteer Cavalry and was the first man of color to serve in the Civil War from Hatboro, Pennsylvania. A 13 November 2013 newspaper article, "Honoring One of Their Own,"[100] was written about him by Phil Gianficaro and published in the *Bucks County Courier Times*. The name was nearly illegible on Sgt. Stagner's tombstone due to weathering and darkening over 148 years. Supplied by the Veterans Administration, a new tombstone was placed a few feet away from the original one.

Because of his light skin color and blue eyes, his mixed race was not known, enabling him to join the Army before Blacks were allowed and later became a sergeant who fought in the Battle of Gettysburg. Upon his re-enlistment as a veteran volunteer, he became a corporal. At age twenty-eight he died on 3 January 1865 outside of Petersburg, Virginia. After being sent to Hatboro, his remains were interred in the cemetery as are his mother's.

Ethel M. Washington, in her book about Union County's Black soldiers,[101] discusses how the tombstones of the United States Colored Troops are identified by the carved letters U.S.C.T. or U.S.C.I. for members of the Infantry. The tombstones of the Blacks who served in white regiments are not so easily found. Certainly race is not evident unless the name is one like that of Scipio Africanus of the 12th New Hampshire Infantry Co I.

She writes, ***"the contributions of most of these soldiers came to light after extensive examination of Union County burial records at the Union County Office of Veterans Affairs in Elizabeth."*** [102]

So it is with the tombstones of unidentified Black soldiers across the country. Consider the tombstone of Crowder Patience who served with the 103rd Pennsylvania Volunteers. Who would know it is the tombstone of a Black Civil War veteran, the only one in the small West Pittston Cemetery? Possibly only descendants and locals who know of the Patience family that settled in the small borough in 1883.

CHAPTER 10

A GRAVESITE LOST IN NORTH CAROLINA

Still other Black soldiers are buried in unknown spots, perhaps in cemeteries where tombstones have not passed the test of time, are illegible or crumbling, or sunken into the ground.

Pvt. Thomas Patience 5th Massachusetts Cavalry is one such soldier whose exact burial site is unknown in Chowan County, North Carolina. Not in the Edenton old Black cemetery or the later public cemetery or among the weathered tombstones behind the church where he had been married.

NORTH CAROLINA STATE BOARD OF HEALTH
BUREAU OF VITAL STATISTICS
STANDARD CERTIFICATE OF DEATH

435

Registration District No. 21-5260
Full name: Thomas Patience
Sex: Male — Color or Race: col — Single, Married, Widowed, or Divorced: Widowed
Date of Birth: Dec 24 1835
Age: 93 years, 11 months, 22 days
Occupation: Common Laborer
Birthplace: Chowan Co
Name of Father: Dont Know
Birthplace of Father: Dont Know
Maiden Name of Mother: Hester Lawrence
Birthplace of Mother: Chowan Co
Informant: Cornelia Lawrence, Edenton N.C.
Filed: Jan 30 — Mrs. H. C. Jackson, Registrar

MEDICAL CERTIFICATE OF DEATH
Date of Death: Dec 23 1929
I HEREBY CERTIFY, That I attended deceased from Nov 1929 to Dec 1929
The CAUSE OF DEATH was as follows: Chronic Arterial Sclerosis, Senility
(Signed) C. P. Williams, M.D.
12/31 1929 (Address) Edenton N.C.
Place of Burial: Chowan Co — Date of Burial: Dec 24 1929
Undertaker: Willie Bembry, Edenton N.C.

Certificate of death of Thomas Patience
(Courtesy of Earl Ijames)

VOLUNTEER ENLISTMENT.

STATE OF ~~TOWN~~ OF

Massachusetts City of Roxbury

I, Thomas D. Patience born in Chowan Co. in the State of North Carolina aged Twenty-four years, and by occupation a Farmer Do hereby acknowledge to have volunteered this Thirteenth day of May 1864, to serve as a Soldier in the Army of the United States of America, for the period of *THREE YEARS*, unless sooner discharged by proper authority: Do also agree to accept such bounty, pay, rations, and clothing, as are, or may be, established by law for volunteers. And I, Thomas D. Patience do solemnly swear, that I will bear true faith and allegiance to the United States of America, and that I will serve them honestly and faithfully against all their enemies or opposers whomsoever; and that I will observe and obey the orders of the President of the United States, and the orders of the officers appointed over me, according to the Rules and Articles of War.

Sworn and subscribed to, at Boston Mass this Thirteenth day of May 1864, Thomas D. his X mark Patience
Before Geo H Deline Witness
Justice of the Peace

I CERTIFY, ON HONOR, That I have carefully examined the above-named Volunteer, agreeably to the General Regulations of the Army, and that, in my opinion, he is free from all bodily defects and mental infirmity, which would in any way disqualify him from performing the duties of a soldier.

B. Joy Jeffries
Examining Surgeon.

Vaccinated

I CERTIFY, ON HONOR, That I have minutely inspected the Volunteer, Thomas D. Patience

Pvt. Thomas Patience

5th Massachusetts Cavalry

Volunteer Enlistment

The name Thomas Patience was unknown to the Patiences of West Pittston, Pennsylvania. As far as they were concerned, their family had begun with the marriage of Crowder and Elsie Veden on 4 August 1874, in Mechanicsburg, Pennsylvania. Not until the fourth generation by DNA testing were we to know that our paternal line can actually be traced back to Cameroon.

How then was Pvt. Thomas Patience discovered by our family who may be, perhaps, his collateral descendants? It happened by a trip to the Wall of Honor surrounding the "Spirit of Freedom," in Washington, D.C.

The bronze monument had been unveiled in July 1998, but the Wall of Honor had not been completed until months later. I had been at the unveiling of the monument, but had not returned to view the Wall of Honor because, disappointingly to me, my great-grandfather's name was not there. Neither his nor other forgotten Black soldiers who had not served in the U.S.C.T. and other segregated regiments. On the Wall, however, is inscribed the name of my stepmother's grandfather, Samuel James Patterson.

I did intend that sometime in the future I would visit the monument to pay homage to the names on the Wall. The time came unexpectedly some months later, when Christine Patterson, great-granddaughter of Samuel J., came to D.C. for business. She asked me if I would take her to see her ancestor's name on the Wall of Honor. Of course, I would be delighted to do so.

We travelled to the Shaw Station via the Metro, escalating up out of the bowels of the earth into the bright sunlight of U Street (near Vermont Avenue NW). The sight of the magnificent eleven foot shiny bronze monument immediately greeted us as our feet rolled off the last step of the steep escalator. There on three sides surrounding the monument is a wall of stainless steel plates, each with an engraved name of a Black soldier or a white officer.

Since the names of the men within each regiment of the U.S.C.T. are placed in alphabetical order, we found in the 5th Massachusetts Cavalry the name--Samuel Patterson. His descendant was delighted to see her Grandpa Patterson's name, and I was glad to be there with her.

Solely because I am a curious person, I suppose, my eyes shifted to the left just to read some of the other names and what did my wandering eyes behold? The name "***Thomas Patience***," also a member of the 5th Massachusetts Cavalry.

What? Who is he? A Black Patience I don't know anything about? I knew that I would eventually want to research his records, but with all that I was doing at the time, I had to put Thomas on the "back burner" with expectations of researching him sometime in the near future.

Two years had passed when I was in Ft. Wayne, Indiana, where the Allen County Library had the second largest genealogical repository after Salt Lake City. That was the first time I had seen *Ancestry.com* on a computer. Excited, I decided while I was there to look for Thomas Patience's military records. After asking where the records of the 5th Massachusetts Colored Cavalry were stored, I was directed to a wooden cabinet containing rolls of microfilm documenting Civil War military records.

After locating the 5th Massachusetts Cavalry, I carefully threaded the microfilm and scrolled to Thomas's records. And what did my wandering eyes behold this time? Twenty-four year-old Thomas Patience had been born in Chowan County, North Carolina, exactly the same place as my ancestor, Crowder Patience. Could the two possibly have been brothers?

I became very excited as I continued reading Thomas's record. I learned that after his enlistment in Norfolk, Virginia, he was sent to Roxbury, Massachusetts, to be mustered into the 5th Massachusetts Colored Cavalry.

After discovering that information, I knew that I needed to find out all I could about him. So I wrote to Broadfoot Publishers in Wilmington, North Carolina, to request copies of his pension papers. However, I did not know if there were any since every veteran had not been able to get the coveted pension. Fortunately, Thomas had and I learned a great deal more about him through the affidavits presented on his behalf.

First of all, I learned that after the war he had returned to Chowan County. Years later he applied for a pension because he had developed rheumatism, was almost blind, and prone to epilepsy, making him unfit for work. In order to survive, he requested the financial assistance the government was providing veterans of the Civil War.

The physical description of Thomas Patience was that of a thin dark-complexioned white haired old man. The same description applied to Crowder Patience. In one of his interviews Thomas stated that his surname was that of his father's. On some military records it was spelled "Pashons," just as it sounds. Nowhere is the spelling "Pacien," though, like Crowder's.

Also he revealed the name of the farm on which he was born. I tried to interpret the name of the farm, but the fancy 19th century handwriting on the pension application was quite illegible to me. All that I could make out was that the name began with a "B" with four or five letters following. It was no name recognizable to me.

So I mailed a copy of the page to my librarian friend, Rosalie Miller, in Edenton, N.C. She could not decipher the name, either. Consequently, I had to wait until I was to visit Edenton once again. That opportunity came during August 2004.

At that time I took the page to the Edenton Courthouse to see if anyone there might be able to read the name of the farm because I felt that if Thomas had been born there, so might

Crowder have been. However, the name was undecipherable to everyone at the courthouse, too.

Act of February 6, 1907.

Declaration for Pension.

The Pension Certificate SHOULD NOT Be Forwarded With the Application.

State of North Carolina
County of Chowan } ss.

On this 4 day of March, A. D. one thousand nine hundred and Seven personally appeared before me, a Notary Public within and for the county and State aforesaid, Thomas Patience, who, being duly sworn according to law, declares that he is 68 YEARS OF AGE, and resident of near Edenton county of Chowan, State of N C; and that he is the identical person who was ENROLLED at Norfolk Va under the name of Thomas Patience, on the — day of April, 1864 as a private, in Co B 5th Mass col vol cav (Here state rank, and company and regiment in the Army, or vessels if in the Navy.) in the service of the United States, in the Civil war (State name of war, Civil or Mexican.) war, and was HONORABLY DISCHARGED at Boston Mass., on the — day of September, 1866. That he also served — (Here give a complete statement of all other services, if any.)

That he has not been employed in the military or naval service of the United States except as stated above. That his personal description at enlistment was as follows: Height, 5 feet 7 inches; complexion, Dark; color of eyes, Black; color of hair, Black; that his occupation was farm hand; that he was born November, 1838
* at Breoles farm near Edenton NC

That his several places of residence since leaving the service have been as follows: in Chowan County NC no where else (State date of each change, as nearly as possible.)

That he is not a pensioner by Certificate No. — at $ — per month. That

Briols misspelled as "Breoles" farm near Edenton, N.C.
Excerpt of Declaration for Pension

Act of February 6, 1907

Declaration for Pension

State of North Carolina
County of Chowan

On this 4 day of March, A.D. one thousand nine hundred and Seven personally appeared before me a Notary Public within and for the country and State aforesaid, Thomas Patience, who, being duly sworn according to law, declares that he is 68 years of age, and resident of near Edenton county of Chowan, State of NC; and that he is the identical person who was enrolled at Norfolk Va under the name of Thomas

Patience, on the ---- day of April, 1864 as a private, in Co B 5th Mass Col.Vol Cav in the service of the United States, in the Civil War, and was honorably disharged at Boston, Mass., on the ----day of September, 1866
That he also served________________
That he has not been employed in the military or naval service of the United States except as stated above.
That his personal description at enlistment was as follows: Height 5 feet 7 inches; complexion Dark, color of eyes, Black, color of hair, Black; that his occupation was farm hand; that he was born November 1838 at Breoles farm near Edenton, NC.

A suggestion was made that we should look in the deed books from 1750-1850 to see if we could find a four or five lettered name beginning with "B." We found it easily. Briols, misspelled on Thomas's pension application as Breoles, the name we could not read. Now I knew where one of the Patience men had been born.

Next I wanted to know just who had been the owner of the farm. The deed indicates that his name was Jean Francois Jably de Briols from Guadeloupe in the West Indies. A Frenchman who had come to the United States hoping to make a fortune, probably in rice production as a number of other West Indian planters had. However, when that did not materialize, he and his wife returned to Guadeloupe in 1803. Until 1890 the property was in the possession of John Coffield and his descendants.

Even after the farm was sold, the name by which it originally had been called remained: Briols. Therefore, when Thomas was asked where he had been born, the recorder spelled the name of the farm as he thought he was hearing pronounced as- "Breoles."

Name:	**Thomas Patience**
Side:	Union
Regiment State/Origin:	Massachusetts
Regiment Name:	5 Mass. Cav. (Col'd.)
Regiment Name Expanded:	5th Regiment, Massachusetts Cavalry (Colored)
Company:	B
Rank In:	Private
Rank In Expanded:	Private
Rank Out:	Private
Rank Out Expanded:	Private
Alternate Name:	Thomas D./Patience
Film Number:	M589 roll 67
Memorial:	Part of the African American Civil War Memorial
Plaque Number:	E-152
Displayed As:	Thomas Patience

103

After the war had ended, Thomas worked as a farm hand until he no longer was able to, hence the need for the pension. On his application Thomas gave his Post Office address as Clum, North Carolina, perhaps not a town, I have been told, but probably just a mail station. It was located about three miles north of Edenton.

Due to the information stated on his pension records, I set out to locate the Briols farm.[103] The original farmhouse still stands on the property from which Thomas, and perhaps Crowder, had absconded in order to gain their freedom by enlisting in the Union Army. The name of a road originally called Briols today is called Brayhall. Both names are found on old maps.

An interesting aside is the fact that the affidavit had been signed by the great-great grandfather of one of the women helping me there at the courthouse. His name had been signed as W. R. Brothers. She told me his full name was William Riley Brothers.

What an exciting moment for his descendant, for while she was helping me, she was thrilled at seeing her own ancestor's contribution so many years ago.

Act of February 6, 1907.

Declaration for Pension.

The Pension Certificate SHOULD NOT Be Forwarded With the Application.

State of North Carolina } ss.
County of Chowan

On this 4 day of March, A. D. one thousand nine hundred and Seven personally appeared before me, a Notary Public within and for the county and State aforesaid, Thomas Patience, who, being duly sworn according to law, declares that he is 68 YEARS OF AGE, and resident of near Edenton, county of Chowan, State of N C; and that he is the identical person who was ENROLLED at Norfolk Va under the name of Thomas Patience, on the — day of April, 1864 as a private, in Co B 5th Mass col vol cav (Here state rank, and company and regiment in the Army, or vessels if in the Navy.)

in the service of the United States, in the Civil War (State name of war, Civil or Mexican.) war, and was HONORABLY DISCHARGED at Boston Mass., on the — day o September, 1866

That he also served — (Here give a complete statement of all other services, if any.)

That he has not been employed in the military or naval service of the United States except as stated above. That his personal description at enlistment was as follows: Height, 5 feet, 7 inches; complexion, dark; color of eyes, Black; color of hair, Black; that his occupation was farm hand; that he was born November, 1838 at Arcale farm near Edenton NC

That his several places of residence since leaving the service have been as follows: in Chowan County NC no where else (State date of each change, as nearly as possible.)

That he is not a pensioner by Certificate No. —, at $ — per month. That he has heretofore applied for pension, Claim No. 1126179

That he makes this declaration for the purpose of being placed on the pension roll of the United States under the provisions of the act of February 6, 1907, and any amendments thereof.

He hereby appoints, with full power of substitution, **EDGAR T. GADDIS**, of Washington, D. C., his successors or legal representatives, his true and lawful attorney to prosecute his claim under said law; and he requests and directs that he be allowed and paid, upon the issuance of a certificate, or thereafter, such fee or compensation as may be hereafter provided by law or ruling.

That his post-office address is Edenton, county of Chowan, State of N C

Thomas his mark Pateince (Claimant's signature in full.)

Attest: (1) W R Brothers
(2) A. A. Johnston

Also personally appeared W R Brothers, residing in Edenton NC and AA Johnson, residing in Edenton NC, persons whom I certify to be respectable and entitled to credit, and who, being by me duly sworn, say that they were present and saw Thomas Patience, the claimant, sign his name (or make his mark) to the foregoing declaration; that they have every reason to believe, from the appearance of the claimant and their acquaintance with him of one years and one years, respectively, that he is the identical person he represents himself to be, and that they have no interest in the prosecution of this claim.

W R Brothers
A. A. Johnston
(Signatures of witnesses.)

SUBSCRIBED and sworn to before me this 4 day of Mch, A. D. 1907.

Declaration for Thomas Patience Pension

Affidavit signed by W. R. Brothers

CERTIFICATE OF HONOR

Thomas Patience

5th **Regiment,** Massachusetts Cavalry (Colored)

Organized at Camp Meigs, Readville. 1st Battalion moved to Washington, D. C., May 5-8, 1864. This name may be located on Wall E, Plaque 152 on the Wall of Honor at the African American Civil War Monument. This monument is located at the intersection of 10th and U Street N.W., Washington, D.C.

A grateful nation finally pays tribute to the 209,145 troops who helped save the nation, end slavery and start America on a struggle for freedom that continues today.

Dr. Frank Smith, Founding Director
Civil War Memorial Freedom Foundation

For more information about this soldier, please visit our website at www.afroamcivilwar.org. You may also wish to search the database for your family name.

Certificate of Honor [104]
Pvt. Thomas Patience
5th Massachusetts Cavalry
One of the 209,145 names on the Wall of Honor

CHAPTER 11

ONE DESCENDANT'S DETERMINATION

Through the years, bits and pieces of information were stored in my mind because I was forever asking questions. To many of them, my Great-Aunt Lillie would say, "Juanita, we didn't ask our parents questions like that."

Her parents, though, had shared where each of them had grown up: her father Crowder, as a slave on a farm near Edenton, North Carolina, and her mother Elsie, as a "bound girl"[105] in Dillsburg, Pennsylvania. Each of their eight children knew exactly where he or she had been born, the last five in West Pittston. They were well aware that their father had been a Civil War soldier because they would watch him as he marched with other veterans on Decoration (Memorial) Day in the annual town parade. After his death, his daughters faithfully decorated their father's grave where a G.A.R. (Grand Army of the Republic) stanchion had been placed and a new American flag was replaced annually on Memorial Day by members of the local American Legion.

Since illiterate ex-slaves could not keep diaries, journals or write letters, they had no way documenting their life's journey. So when they arrived at a place where they might live in peace, they settled in, hoping to remain there until the end of their lives, as did my great-grandfather who died in West Pittston, Pennsylvania, in 1930. Also, most children of ex-slaves were not interested in their parents' former lives in bondage and, besides, the parents did not want to discuss the lives from which they had metamorphosed.

Being far distanced from the South and one of only a few families of Blacks in the small town, the first generation of Patiences knew little about southern culture. Instead, they were reared in a European immigrant community, attended school with white children, and attended a white Presbyterian church until

St. Mark's African Methodist Episcopal Church was built in 1908 after the first generation of Patience children had become adults.

Not one member of the first freeborn generation seemed to have had any interest in finding their father's family with North Carolina being so far away from Pennsylvania. For instance, Aunt Lillie knew nothing about her father's family members. That is, not to say there were none, but she told me that her father never spoke of any. Besides, as Aunt Lillie kept reminding me, children of that era did not question their parents much.

Some members of the third generation had some interest in their ancestry. Having been educated in the public schools where they had studied American history, they became curious. I know that at least two of my grandfather Harry's sons, Robert and Kenneth, had asked their grandfather questions.

Furthermore, Uncle Bob's name can be read on a "sign-in" record at the National Archives. Two years after his grandfather's death in 1930, Uncle Bob had studied the records of Private Crowder Patience, 103rd Pennsylvania Volunteers. Sometime in the 1960's, Uncle Bob gave me a copy of a 1928 *Sunday Independent* article written about Grandpa two years before his death. I was thrilled to receive it, even though I was not able to see the details of the photograph since copying quality in those days left much to be desired. That article, however, was to provide me with a basis on which to build my novel, ***Created to Be Free***, forty years later.

Uncle Kenneth's daughter added an interesting anecdote to the family history. She said that her father had told her that Grandpa's owner was a French man from the West Indies.

Much oral history is considered folklore because the whole truth is not known. For instance, other stories were passed along like Uncle Bob's telling me that Grandpa got his name of Patience when he was in the war because he was so "patient." In ***Created to Be Free*** I state that some of what I have written may very well be folklore. Since so little is known about my great-grandfather, I could not write his biography. Any of the people I could have interviewed in order to learn more about him are no longer living.

What truth I know about Crowder Pacien (Patience), I have included under the "Facts" in ***Created to Be Free***. His military records state that he was from Chowan County, North Carolina, about which I knew absolutely nothing. Before completing the book, I felt that I had to go to North Carolina to view the terrain there in October. Since my great grandfather enlisted on 1 January 1864, he had to have absconded prior to that date. October may have been the month since the harvesting would have been completed, the nights had become longer, and the weather had not yet turned cold.

According to Uncle Bob, Grandpa had said his slave name had been "Toby." The renowned African American historian John Hope Franklin described a typical absconding slave in a book about runaways. [106] He was a dark-skinned teen-aged field hand. Like many slaves, my ancestor had but one name —his slave name and no surname. On his enlistment record, though, he had somehow become "Crowder Pacien." Two names for a free man who would one day settle his family in Northeastern Pennsylvania. How those names were chosen, I do not know.

The next generation of Patiences knew only themselves. They had no relatives on either side of the family, but Crowder had told his children that he was from "Edington," North Carolina. He and Elsie were the beginning of the Colored Patiences in Pennsylvania. Were there others? The family had no idea and had no way to find out until some of the descendants began to travel out of Wyoming Valley.

For instance, my father, Charles Edgar Patience, liked to check telephone books on his travels to see if any Patiences were listed. He was curious, but even if he should find a name, he never would make a call.

Once when I saw a Patience listed in *Who's Who Among College and University Students*, I was curious enough to call the number. I learned that the family had originated in Cornwall, England, where I was told there were many Patiences. So then I knew we were not the only Patiences in the world. However, I still wondered if we were the only Black Patiences.

When I traveled to Edenton, North Carolina, in 2000 for the first time, attempting to find the farm from which Grandpa had absconded, I came up empty-handed. The name Pacien or any spelling of Patience is nowhere to be found in Chowan County. So I presumed the trail had ended. However, one day I was going to be pleasantly surprised.

People who have read my books know that my research began with the unveiling of the "Spirit of Freedom" monument in Washington, D.C., on 18 July 1998. I became aware, by attending a symposium in July 1998, that Black soldiers who were not in the USCT, but in white regiments were not being acknowledged. No one was aware of any such soldiers, including respected historians. The only reason I was privy to the fact is because my great-grandfather is one of those forgotten men.

Information concerning their role in the war had not been in print until the publication in 2004 of my small tome, ***Forgotten Black Soldiers Who Served in White Regiments During the Civil War***. In it I listed the 1,000 names I had discovered. That list was not complete, I knew, but the number was enough to hypothetically fill an additional regiment of Black soldiers. In 2008 my revised book listed 2,000 names. The number continues to rise with additional names provided by interested and enthusiastic correspondents, new authors, and *Ancestry.com*.

CONCLUSION

Family stories passed to the next generation may become inflated, filtered, or diminished as memory fades into time. Censuses, military records, and newspaper articles may have some truth; however, they, too, may become inflated, filtered, or diminished. Of utmost importance to "family griots"[107] like myself, is to try to get as much truth as possible. So it may have to be with military records.

Suppose family lore contains a Civil War veteran about whom very little is known. I have attempted in my two volumes to explain how I have found as much as I have about our family without known roots. Our slave ancestor reinvented himself in northeastern Pennsylvania. Whatever memories he had about his slave family he did not share. Unfortunately, when descendants like myself four generations later are at the point in our evolution to accept the truth about Grandpa's early life, albeit how bitter and degrading, very little is known. He probably had not even shared with his much younger free-born wife.

In order to help other descendants who have heard that they have Civil War ancestors, but do not know how to go about finding them, I have attempted to help them along their path to truth. If they go to the "Spirit of Freedom" in Washington, D.C., and do not see their ancestor's name on the "Wall of Honor," they will think the family lore is false. That may not be true, since he may have been one of the many Black soldiers who have been forgotten by history.

Ancestry.com is a wonderful source of family history and military information. Before the records were digitalized, researchers had to toil through the records at the National Archives in Washington, D.C. Now much of that information is just a finger click away.

At the suggestion of historian Geoffrey Sattler, I searched for Black Civil War soldiers on *Ancestry.com* under the singular keywords "undercook," "colored cook," "colored teamster," "colored saddler," and "colored blacksmith." Many names can be found; therefore I have listed just a few in each category so readers will see how the information is recorded.

The following are some suggestions for those readers who are genealogy novices just like I was in 1998. You may not be Civil War "buffs," but are interested in learning more about your ancestry:

1. Talk with the oldest members of your family, as well as close older friends. Record their conversations, if they will allow. Do not make them uncomfortable with your questions.
2. Look through old photograph albums to identify as many persons as possible.
3. Read any records written in family Bibles. Most will be of marriages, births, and deaths.
4. Look at the mementos saved by your ancestors. Some may have a story like my grandfather's Sons of Civil War Veterans pendant which I wear during my presentations.
5. Read obituaries and/or other articles published about family members. One of my great-aunts stored her collection in a teapot.
6. Visit cemeteries to photograph tombstones. Use my suggestions for finding the Civil War graves of Blacks.
7. Study census records in *Ancestry.com* for names of family members and neighbors.
8. Use *Ancestry.com* for military information, including the film number (NARA microfilm series and roll number where soldiers' information is found).
9. Research additional records at the National Archives in Washington, D.C. If you live far distances away from the Nation's Capitol, you may hire professional researchers.

Happy hunting.

ADDITIONAL BLACK SOLDIERS ALPHABETIZED

Abers, Charles	5th Cavalry	NY	Co L
	Blacksmith		
Abbott, Charles	2nd Mounted Rifles	NY	?
	Teamster		
Abbott, Silas	2nd Infantry	MI	Co G
	Teamster		
Abbott, William	100th Infantry	IN	Co B
	Teamster		
Ables, Henry	15th Cavalry	KS	Co L
	Bugler		
Abner, John	75th Infantry	IN	Co C
	Teamster		
Abrams, William	1st Mounted Rifles	NY	Co M
	Teamster		
Abrannum, James	5th Cavalry	MO	Co D
	Blacksmith		
Achison, Thomas	17th	KY	Co K
	Saddler		
Acken, Henry S.	3rd Cavalry	MO	Co E
	Blacksmith		
Acker, George	136th Infantry	PA	Co FH
	Teamster		
Ackerman, Benjamin	28th Infantry	NJ	Co C
Ackerman, George W.	1st Light Art'y	PA	Bat'y F
Ackerman, Phillip	7th Infantry	NJ	Co E
Ackerman, William	22nd Infantry	NJ	Co A
Ackermann, John	5th Cavalry	MO	Co D
	Blacksmith		
Ackles, William	2nd Militia Cav.	MI	Co E
	Saddler		
Acoam, John W.	4th Cavalry	IN	Co G
	Saddler		

Name	Regiment	Branch	State	Company
Acmon/Achmond, James	7th	Cavalry	MO	Co E
	Blacksmith			
Acuff, John T.	1st	Cavalry	IN	Co H
	Blacksmith/Farrier			
Adair, James	16th	Cavalry	NY	Co B
	Teamster			
Adair, Samuel F.	7th	Cavalry	IO	Co L
	Saddler			
Adam, John	1st	Cavalry	MO	Co A
	Blacksmith			
Adams, Adam	4th	Cavalry	MO	Co G
	Blacksmith			
Adams, Anson	108th	Infanty	IL	Co G
	Wagoner			
Adams, Charles	14th	Infantry	NJ	Co C
	Teamster			
Adams, David O.	4th	Cavalry	IN	Co A
	Teamster			
Adams, Davis	5th	Heavy Art'y	RI	Co H
Adams, Ephraim	136th	Infantry	OH	Co E
Adams, Frederick	7th	Infantry	KY	Co E
	Teamster			
Adams, George	95th	Infantry	IL	Co A
	Teamster			
Adams, Jeremiah	128th	Infantry	IL	Co K
	Teamster			
Adams, John	18th	Cavalry	PA	Co M
	Teamster			
Adams, John	19	Infantry	IL	Co F
	Teamster			
Adams, Johnson H.	98th	Infantry	IL	Co F
	Teamster			
Adams, Joshua	2nd	Infantry	MO	?
	Teamster			
Adams, Lorain	16th	Cavalry	NY	G
	Farrier			

Adams, Robert	1st	Infantry	OH	Co I
	Teamster			
Adams, Robert	4th	Cavalry	OH	Ind. Bat'y
	Blacksmith/Farrier			
Adams, Samuel	3rd	Cavalry	OH	Co I
	Teamster			
Adams, Thomas	57th	Infantry	NY	Co D
	Teamster			
Adams, William	160th	Infantry	NY	Co K
Adams, William	Light Art'y		PA	
	Artifer/Blacksmith		100 day 1864	
Adams, William H.	19th	Infantry	OH	Co K
	Teamster			Co EC
Adams, William S.	133rd	Infantry	OH	Co. K
	Teamster			
Adams, William W.	6th	Cavalry	MI	Co H
Adcock, Tom N.	3rd	Cavalry	KY	?
	Blacksmith/Farrier			
Adkins, Jacob	52nd	Infantry	IL	Co F
	Teamster			
Adkins, Peter	133rd	Infantry	NY	Co. F
	Teamster			
Adkinson, John R.	3rd	Cavalry	KY	Co H
	Blacksmith			
Aetheridge, March	89th	Infantry	NY	?
Agnew, James	1st	Cavalry	MN	Co I
Aikin, Alexander M.	100th	Infantry	PA	Co C
	Teamster			
Akerman, Jacob	11th	Cavalry	IL	Co H
	Farrier			
Akers, Joseph	128th	Infantry	IL	Co F
	Teamster			
Alan, Christopher	26th	Infantry	NJ	Co A
Albert, Joseph	8th	Infantry	NH	Co K
Albertson, Samuel W.	23rd	Infantry	PA	Co I
Albright, Homer	38th	Infantry	IL	Co F

Alderman, Bidwell	28th	Infantry	OH	Co I
	Teamster			
Aldrich, Joel	6th	Cavalry	MI	Co M
	Teamster			
Aldrich, Levi	75th	Infantry	OH	Co G
	Teamster			
Aldridge/Aldrich, Wm. B.	105th	Infantry	IL	Co K
	Teamster			
Alexander, Hazem	1st	Infantry	VT	Co E
	Wagoner			
Alexander, James	128th	Infantry	NY	Co G
	Teamster			
Alexander, Joseph	50th	Infantry	NY	Co A
	Teamster			
Alexander, Stevens	78th	Infantry	IL	Co A
Alexander, Thornton	18th	Cavalry	NY	Co H
Alexander, William	35th	Infantry	WI	Co H
Alfred, John	8th	Infantry	NH	Co K
Allan, Andrew	85th	Infantry	IL	Co D
Allberger, William	165th	Infantry	OH	Co F
Allen, Andrew	85th	Infantry	IL	Co D
	Teamster			
Allen, Asbury	142nd	Infantry	NY	Co D
Allen, David	8th	Infantry	WI	Co A
Allen, George	26th	Light Art'y	NY	Ind. Bat'y
Allen, James C.	3rd	Infantry	KY	Co F
	Teamster			
Allen, John	13th	Cavalry	PA	Co F
	Teamster			
Allen, Joseph	21st	Infantry	IO	Co H
	Teamster			
Allen, Samuel	2nd	Cavalry	NE	Co D
	Saddler			
Allen, Warren	52nd	Infantry	IL	Co K
	Teamster			
Allen, William H.	3rd	Infantry	MD	Co F
	Teamster			
Allen, William S.	11th	Infantry	OH	Co K
	Teamster			
Allen, William T.	84th	Infantry	IN	Co K

Alstine, Thomas Van	25th	Infantry	NY	Co I
	Teamster			
Alton/Alten, Henry	4th	Cavalry	MI	Co F
	Teamster			
Ambs, Fred John	52nd	Infantry	NY	Co H
	Teamster			
Ambrooke, Charles	2nd	Cavalry	MI	Co K
	Saddler			
Amburn, Samuel	10th	Cavalry	TN	Co I
	Saddler			
Ambuster, Jacob	5th	Cavalry	PA	Co G
	Saddler			
Amend, Michael	3rd	Cavalry	OH	Co L
	Saddler			
Amos, William	13th	Cavalry	IN	Co I
	Teamster			
Anderson, Carroll	18th	Infantry	IN	Co AC
	Teamster			
Anderson, James	1st	Cavalry	PA	Co C
	Teamster			
Anderson, John	9th	Infantry	NJ	Co A
Anderson, Joseph	21st	Infantry	IO	Co H
	Teamster			
Anderson, Loyal	9th	Cavalry	IL	Co F,E
	Teamster			
Anderson, M. R.	11th	Infantry	NY	Co F
Anderson, Nathan	52nd	Infantry	IL	Co K
Anderson, Nicholas	3rd	Infantry	TN	Co E
	Teamster			
Anderson, Reason T.	13th	Cavalry	IN	Co I
	Saddler			
Anderson, Stewart	2nd	Infantry	NJ	Co D
Anderson, Thomas	3rd	Infantry	NJ	Co A
Andrews, Robert D.	6th	Infantry	IN	Co H
	Teamster			
Angle/Angel, James M.	7th	Infantry	OH	Co I
	Teamster/Farrier			

Name	Regiment		State	Company
Ani, Daniel	14th	Cavalry	NY	Co BA
	Saddler			
Ankeney, Henry	3rd	Cavalry	WV	Co F
	Saddler			
Anthony, Henry	11th	Infantry	NJ	Co
Antrim, Watson	6th Light Artillery		NY Ind. Bat'y	
Apgar, Hulet	31st	Infantry	NJ	Co A
	Teamster			
Appo, William	30th	Infantry	NY	Co I
Appott, August	5th	Cavalry	PA	Co L
	Teamster			
Archer/Archard, L. H.	7th	Cavalry	OH	Co D
	Teamster			
Archibald, Samuel	4th	Cavalry	OH	Co B,D
	Teamster			
Archy, Torian	42nd	Infantry	IL	Co K
Arens, John	94th	Infantry	OH	Co F
	Teamster			
Argenbright, James M.	1st	Cavalry	IN	Co M
	Teamster			
Ark, George	18th	Cavalry	NY	Co B
	Teamster			
Armfield, Herk	19th	Infantry	MI	Co K
	Teamster			
Armitage, Hiram	81st	Infantry	OH	Co A
	Teamster			
Armstead, Willis	52nd	Infantry	IL	Co D
Armstrong, Edward/Edwin	136th	Infantry	OH	Co A
	Teamster			
Arthur, William H.	10th	Cavalry	MO	Co A
	Blacksmith/Farrier			
Artist, Andrew	7th	Cavalry	OH	Co G
	Saddler			
Asberry Allen	142nd	Infantry	NY	Co D
Ash, George	18th	Cavalry	NY	Co B
	Teamster			
Ash, George W.	119th	Infantry	PA	Co D
	Teamster			
Ash, George W.	9th	Infantry	NJ	Co K

Ash, Henry	3rd	Infantry	NJ	Co K
	Ass/t surgeon			
Ash, Jesse B.	122nd	Infantry	IL	Co A
	Teamster			
Ashburn, George W.	6th	Cavalry	IO	Co G
	Teamster			
Asher, Theophilius	14th	Cavalry	KY	Co M
	Teamster			
Assam/Assim/Assem, Louis	4th	Cavalry	OH	Co E,D
Athens/Athons, William	60th	Infantry	IN	Co I
	Teamster			
Atkins, Jacob	52nd	Infantry	IL	Co F
	Teamster			
Atkinson, John R.	3rd	Cavalry	KY	Co A
	Blacksmith/Farrier			
Atkinson, Thomas	1st M'td. Rifles		NY	Co G,E
	Saddler			
Atkinson, William	11th	Cavalry	IN	Co D
	Saddler			
Atskuson, Robert	12th	Cavalry	IL	Co C
	Saddler			
Atterbery, Isaac T.	1st	Cavalry	MO	Co L
	Saddler			
Atwater, John D.	95th	Infantry	IL	Co E
	Teamster			
Atwood/Attwood, Daniel	23rd	Infantry	PA	Co R
	Teamster			
Atwood, Daniel	61st	Infantry	PA	Co I
	Teamster			
Auble, James	6th	Cavalry	MI	Co A
	Teamster			
Ault, William	99th	Infantry	OH	Co K
	Teamster			
Augerger, William	165th	Infantry	OH	?
	Teamster			
Austin, Almzo	7th	Infantry	OH	Co K
	Teamster			

Austin, William	50th	Infantry	NY	Co F
	Teamster			
Avery, George B.	1st	Artillary	NJ	Bat'yD
Avery, Thomas	4th	Infantry	NJ	Co B
Avery, William	30th	Infantry	NJ	Co C
Avory, Thomas W.	13th	Cavalry	TN	Co B
Babbett, Edward	11th	Infantry	CT	Co A
	Teamster			
Babcock, Perry	99th	Infantry	OH	Co C
	Teamster			
Babcock, Sidney M.	57th	Infantry	PA	Co D
	Teamster			
Babcock, William F.	4th	Cavalry	MI	Co E
	Teamster			
Babbett, John C.	11th	Cavalry	IL	Co. F
	Saddler			
Babbitt, James	6th	Cavalry	KS	Co A,E
	Saddler			
Babbitt, Putnam P.	11th	Cavalry	NY	Co G
	Saddler			
Babcock, Alphonzo	3rd	Cavalry	NY	Co D,L
	Saddler			
Bailey, John A.	1st	Cavary	IO	Co K
	Saddler			
Backhouse, Hermann	3rd	Cavalry	MI	Co E
	Teamster			
Backus, Robert	13th	Cavalry	NY	Co F
	Teamster			
Baggs, John	86th	Infantry	IL	Co C
Bagley/Baigley, Joseph	1st	Infantry	OH	Co I
	Teamster			
Bailey/Baily, Edward	14th	Cavalry	IL	Co K
	Teamster			
Bair, Samuel	79th	Infantry	PA	Co C
	Teamster			
Bair, William	80th	Infantry	OH	Co C
	Teamster			

Baird, Robert G.	22nd	Infantry	IL	Co H
	Teamster			
Baits, Abraham	58th	Infantry	IN	Co E
	Teamster			
Baker, Aaron	38th	Infantry	NJ	Co G
Baker, George	7th	Cavalry	MI	Co B
	Teamster			
Baker, George W.	9th	Cavalry	MO	Co G
	Teamster			
Baker, James	11th	Cavalry	KY	Co F
	Teamster			
Baker, James H.	14th	Cavalry	KY	Co G
	Saddler			
Baker, Jeremiah	9th	Cavalry	OH	Co H
	Farrier			
Baker, John	26th	Infantry	NJ	Co K
Baker, John	1st	Cavalry	AK	Co E
	Teamster			
Baker, John	57th	Infantry	OH	Co B
	Teamster			
Baker, John D.	84th	Infantry	PA	Co E
	Teamster			
Baker, Johnathan	4th	Infantry	OH	Co H
	Teamster			
Baker, Levi	59th	Infantry	NY	Co I
	Teamster			
Baker, Nathan	9th	Infantry	MN	Co D
	Teamster			
Baker, Philip	6th	Cavalry	OH	Co B
	Teamster			
Baker, Robinson	136th	Infantry	NY	Co H
	Teamster			
Baker, William	5th	Infantry	NJ	Co F
Baldwin, Byron	27th	Infantry	MI	Co A
	Teamster			
Baldwin, Edward	9th	Infantry	NJ	Co K

Baldwin, George	4th	Infantry	MI	Co K
	Teamster			
Baldwin, John	14th	Infantry	NJ	Co I
Baley, Dock L.	11th	Cavalry	TN	Co C
	Teamster			
Ball, Daniel O.	5th	Cavalry	MO	Co I
	Teamster			
Ballard, Nicholas	4th	Cavalry	OH	Co I
Ballard, Sampson	10th	Cavalry	TN	Co B
	Farrier			
Balleu, Banjamin	3rd	Cavalry	MO	Co B
	Farrier			Co C,D
Balliet, Edward	19th	Cavalry	PA	Co K
	Farrier			
Ballinger, James	5th	Cavalry	MI	Co D
Ballou, Asa	2nd	Cavalry	NY	Co H
	Teamster/Saddler			
Ballou, Henry	22nd	Cavalry	NY	Co M
	Saddler			
Ballsover, Alfred	1st	Cavalry	IN	Co B
	Saddler			
Bancum, Samuel	12th	Cavalry	KY	Co G
	Teamster			
Banger, John	11th	Infantry	MO	Co D
	Teamster			
Bannister, Robert C.	15th	Cavalry	KY	Co D
	Teamster			
Bansing/Benton, Carlos C.	10th	Cavalry	OH	Co G
	Teamster			
Barber, Peter	114th	Infantry	IN	Co I
	Teamster			
Barbero, John, Jr.	86th	Infantry	IL	Co F
	Teamster			
Barbra/Barlrey/Peter	144th	Infantry	IN	Co I
	Teamster			
Bare, Samuel	79th	Infantry	PA	Co C

Barefoot/Barfoot, Edward	4th	Cavalry	OH	Co B
	Teamster			
Barger, John F.	13th	Infantry	MD	Co D
	Teamster			
Barkalew, Vincent	3rd	Infantry	NJ	Co I
	Teamster			
Barker, John	1st	Cavalry	OH	Co B
	Farrier			
Barker, John H.	12th	Cavalry	OH	Co C
	Saddler			
Barker, Samuel	3rd	Cavalry	NY	Co H
	Saddler			
Barnett, James B.	16th	Cavalry	KS	Co C,I
	Farrier			
Barrett, Daniel	1st	Cavalry	IL	Co C
	Blacksmith/Farrier			
Barrows, William P.	5th	Cavalry	MI	Co L
	Farrier			
Bartholamew, Daniel	17th	Cavalry	PA	Co K
	Saddler			
Bartholemew, Ephraim	2nd	Cavalry	PA	Co F
	Saddler			
Bauer, George	1st	Cavalry	NJ	Co C
Baumann, Louis	4th	Cavalry	OH	Co E
	Teamster			
Baumgardner, Absalom	4th	Cavalry	PA	Co H
	Farrier			
Baumgardner, Isaiah	8th	Cavalry	OH	Co A
	Farrier			
Baumgardner, Henry	10th	Cavalry	OH	Co A
	Farrier			
Baurs, Jacob	4th	Cavalry	MI	Co D
	Teamster			
Bawker/Boker, Oscar P.	9th	Cavalry	OH	Co G
	Teamster			
Baxter, Gilbert	7th	Cavalry	PA	Co C
	Saddler			

Bayer/Boyer, Henry M.	9th Cavalry Teamster	OH	Co G
Bayless, Platt	11th Cava;ry Teamster	IN	Co H
Bayly, Dock L.	4th Cavalry Teamster	IN	Co E
Beam/Beans, Aaron	49TH Infantry Teamster	IN	Co B
Beam, Daniel	101st Infantry Teamster	PA	Co D
Beam, Daniel	55th Infantry Teamster	PA	?
Beam, Jesse L.	15th Cavalry Teamster	KY	Co A
Beam, Robert C.	14th Cavalry Teamster	PA	Co D
Bear, Samuel	79th Cavalry Teamster	PA	Co C
Bearach, William	23rd Infantry Teamster	IN	Co A
Beath, Edward	5th Cavalry Saddler	IL	Co C
Beatty/Beaty, William V.	81st Infantry Teamster	OH	Co G
Beatty, Wilson	4th Cavalry Teamster	OH	Co D,I
Beck, Henry R.	23rd Infantry Teamster	PA	Co A
Becknell, William H.	14th Cavalry Teamster	KY	Co F
Beckwith, John	8th Infantry Teamster	MI	Co C
Bedgar, John	17th Infantry Teamster	PA	Co E
Bedlow, John	124th Cavalry Teamster	PA	Co F

Beeken, William	1st Mounted Rifles Blacksmith/Farrier	NY	Co L
Beezely/Beezly, Nathaniel	2nd Cavalry Farrier	IN	Co B
Beggs, James	5thI. Batt'yCavalry Blacksmith/Farrier	OH	Co A
Begley, Asa	14th Cavalry Teamster	KY	Co M
Beh, Benedict	6th Cavalry Saddler	IO	Co HF
Behrens, Henry	1st Light Art'y Farrier	IL	Co H
Beird, Henry C.	7th Cavalry Saddler	MI	Co L
Beirtling, Charles	7th Cavalry Saddler	MO S.M	Co FA
Bell, Thomas, Jr.	2nd Cavalry Saddler	IO	Co K
Bennett, Charles	7th Cavalry Farrier	IN	Co I,A
Bennett, George H.	10th Cavalry Farrier	MI	Co K
Bennett, George W.	6th Light Artillery	NY	Ind. Bat'y
Bennett, John R.	22nd Infantry	NJ	Co A
Benson, Charles	34th Infantry	NJ	Co A
Berg, Adam	5th Cavalry Farrier	MO	Co A
Bergman, Godfrey/Gotfred	7th Infantry Teamster	NY	Co A
Berlew, Jonathan	116th Infantry Teamster	IL	Co H
Bertram, Peter	208th Infantry Teamster	PA	Co B
Berthold, Adler	3rd Provincial Cav. Farrier	NY	Co L
Bierly/Birely, Oliver	1st Cavalry Farrier	OH	Co I

Biermann, Louis	13th Farrier	Cavalry	IL	Co C
Biggers, Aaron	52nd	Infantry	IL	Co I
Birkhall, Francis P.	1st Farrier	Cavalry	IO	Co H
Birt, Andrew	3rd Teamster	Cavalry	IN	Co L
Bischer, Eliphalet	5th Teamster	Infantry	NY	Co C
Bishop, Abner	12th Saddler	Cavalry	TN	Co F
Bishop, Cleveland	7th Saddler	Cavalry	IN	Co AC
Bishop, James C.	21st Saddler	Cavalry	PA	Co G
Bishop, William	6th Light Artillery		NY Ind. Bat'y	
Blackson, James C.	11th Saddler	Cavalry	IL	Co C
Bolen, Benjamin	85th Teamster	Infantry	IL	Co H
Bonebright/Bonebrite, Jacob	7th Farrier	Cavalry	MO	Co M
Boots, Jacob	9th Farrier	Cavalry	KY	Co C
Borkhous, William	2nd Saddler	Cavalry	IL	Co G
Borland, James W.	23rd Teamster	Infantry	PA	Co K
Bowan, James	7th Saddler	Cavalry	IN	Co E
Bowman, John	4th Teamster	Cavalry	OH	Co E
Bown, Henry	52nd	Infantry	IL	Co G
Boyer, George	110th Teamster	Infantry	PA	Co G
Boyer, George	105th Teamster	Infantry	PA	Co I

Boyer, Henry	9th	Cavalry	PA	Co G
	Teamster			
Braden, Porter	50th	Infantry	IL	Co D
Bradley, William	18th	Cavalry	KS	Co. B
	Saddler			
Bradley, William	6th	Cavalry	TN	Co B
	Teamster			
Brady, James	118th	Infantry	NY	Co C
Brady, Samuel	118th	Infantry	NY	Co C
Branch/Brunt, George W.	6th	Light Artillery	NY	Ind. Bat'y
Branch/Brunt, Harvey	6th	Light Artillery	NY	Ind. Bat'y
Brandt, Henry	54th	Infantry	NY	?
Brasch, John	3rd	Cavalry	WI	Co M
	Saddler			
Breysacher, John	1st	Cavalry	MO	Co KC
	Saddler			
Briant, William C.	7th	Cavalry	KS	Co H
	Saddler			
Brill, George W.	8th	Infantry	NJ	Co I
Brinkerhoff, George A.	22nd	Infantry	NJ	Co A
Brinkerhoff, John D.	22nd	Infantry	NJ	Recruit
Brody, Alexander	165	Infantry	NY	Co C
Brokaw, Edwin	37th	Infantry	NJ	Co C
Brokaw, Isaac I.	3rd	Infantry	NJ	Co I
Brown, Alexander	11th	Infantry	NJ	Co D
Brown, Charles M.	9th	Infantry	NJ	Co K
Brown, George Henry	6th	Light Artillery	NY	Ind. Bat'y
Brown, George Washington	6th	Light Artillery	NY	Ind. Bat'y
Brown, Harrison	2nd	Cavalry	NE Territory	Co D
Brown, Henry	9th	Infantry	NJ	Co C
Brown, James	74th	Infantry	IN	Co C
Brown, Joe	43rd	Infantry	IL	Co K
Brown, John	50th	Infantry	IL	Co K
Brown, Milton A.	100th	Infantry	OH	Co E
Brown, Peter	164th	Infantry	NY	Co H
Brown, William D.	81st	Infantry	IL	Co G
	Teamster			

Brown, William H.	2nd Cavalry Saddler	PA	Co G,E
Brum, Ira	185th Infantry	NY	Co F
Bruster, John	33rd Infantry Teamster	OH	Co A
Brusweller, Harrison	10th Cavalry Saddler	IL	Co A
Brutchey, Joseph E.	13th Infantry Teamster	MD	Co B
Buck, John T.	1st Cavalry Saddler	NJ	Co A
Buck, Julius	10th Cavalry Saddler	IL	Co CA
Buckbee, James A.	2nd Cavalry Saddler	WV	Co I
Buckhardt, Henry	5th Cavalry Saddler	OH	Co D
Bucknells, James	115th Infantry Teamster	IL	Co D
Bullman, John	14th Cavalry Saddler	PA	Co L
Bullmer, William	1st Prov'l Cavalry Saddler	PA	Co K
Bulmer, William	20th Cavalry Saddler	PA	Co K
Bulsover, Alfred	1st Cavalry Saddler	IN	Co B
Bulstein, Nicholas	23rd Cavalry Saddler	NY	Co A
Buman/Beeman, Joel S.	2nd Cavalry Saddler	MI	Co F
Bumgardner, Jefferson	9th Cavalry Teamster	IN	Co KA
Burghhardt, Henry	5th Cavalry Saddler	OH	Co D
Buris, Charles	80th Infantry Teamster	IN	Co B

Burns, James	16th	Cavalry	PA	Co B
	Teamster			
Burns, James J.	6th	Cavalry	KY	Co G
	Saddler			
Burton, David	12th	Cavalry	KY	Co LEC
	Teamster			
Butler, Barkley	141st	Infantry	OH	Co F
	Teamster			
Butler, Benjamin I.	19th	Cavalry	PA	Co C
	Saddler			
Caine, Edmond	5th	Cavalry	OH	Co F
	Saddler			
Cakarice, Michael	1st	Cavalry	MD	Co B
	Farrier			
Capp, John M.	132nd	Infantry	PA	Co K
	Teamster			
Caldwell, James	15th	Cavalry	PA	Co B
	Farrier			
Calhoun, Thomas C.	7th	Cavalry	TN	Co I
	Farrier			
Calkins, James	13th	Cavalry	NY	Co E,K
	Farrier			
Calkins, James	3rd	Cavalry Prov.	NY	Co K
Callaghan, Michael F.	2nd	Cavalry	CA	Co M
	Farrier			
Calvin, George W.	3rd	Cavalry	MO	Co F
	Farrier			
Calvin, Horace	10th	Cavalry	MO	Co. C
	Farrier			
Cameron, Archibald	5th	Cavalry	OH	Co K
	Farrier			
Cameron, James	3rd	Cavalry	NY	Co E
	Farrier			
Carle, Thomas	52nd	Infantry	NY	Co B
Carman, Daniel V.	5th	Infantry	NJ	Co H
Carolina, Lecrett	1st	Engineers	NY	Co H
Carr, Berry	22nd	Infantry	IN	Co G

Carr, Jacob	82nd	Infantry	IN	Co F
Carroll, Robert	U.S.	Army	Hospital Steward	
Carter, John W.	3rd	Infantry	NC	Co D
	Teamster		Mounted	
Cary, Anson	6th	Cavalry	MI	Co M
	Teamster			
Cary, Hiram	8th	Cavalry	MI	Co M
	Teamster			
Case, Daniel W.	2nd	Cavalry	NE	Co A
	Teamster			
Chamberlain, Edmond D.	51st	Infantry	MA	Co E B
Chamberlain, Wm. Conner	23rd	Infantry	MA	Co D
Champion, John G.	12th	Infantry	NJ	Co I
Cherry, John	12th	Cavalry	KY	Co F
	Teamster			
Chester, Washington	26	Ind. Battery	NY	?
Chew, William H.	9th	Infantry	NJ	Co K
Clark, Felix	87th	Infantry	IL	Co K
	Teamster			
Clark, Isaac	3rd	Infantry	NJ	Co A
Clark, John R.	22nd	Infantry	NJ	Co A
Clark, Moses P.	6th Light Artillery		NY Ind. Bat'y	
Clark, Robert	8th	Infantry	NJ	Co I
Clark, Thomas	14th	Infantry	NJ	Co E
Clines, Jacob	137th	Infantry	IN	Co I
	Teamster			
Clinger/Clingle, John	66th	Infantry	IL	Co E,B
	Teamster			
Clingle, Samuel	56th	Infantry	OH	Co E,B
	Teamster			
Cochrane, William H.	33rd	Infantry	NJ	Co K
Colby, James	54th	Infantry	OH	Co B
Cole, Jabez C.	52nd	Infantry	PA	Co I
Collins, John	98th	Infantry	IL	Co E
	Teamster			
Collins, Isaac	38th	Infantry	WI	Co H
Connelly, Michael	9th	Infantry	NJ	Co G

Connett, Johnathan T.	30th	Infantry	NJ	Co H
Conour, John	60th	Infantry	IL	Co F
	Teamster			
Conover, Jacob	9th	Infantry	NJ	Co G
Conover, Samuel	28th	Infantry	NJ	Co C
Conover, William W.	14th	Infantry	NY	Co I
Conroy, John	9th	Infantry	NJ	Co K
Cook, Alfred	9th	Infantry	NJ	Co B
Cook, Charles	9th	Infantry	NJ	Co A
Cook, James	9th	Infantry	NJ	Co K
Cook, Peter	11th	Infantry	NJ	Co B
Cook, William	1st	Cavalry	NJ	Co C
Cooley, James	3rd	Cavalry	NJ	Co F
Cooper, Abraham	53rd	Infantry (1st)	NY	Co H
	Teamster			
Corcoran, John	9th	Infantry	NJ	Co K
Cosgrove, William	Smith's Ind'pt	Cavalry	MD	?
	Teamster			
Coslow, Marion	4th	Infantry	KY	Co F
	Teamster		Mounted	
Costello, Edward	66th	Infantry	PA	Co K
	Teamster			
Cowdon, James Seneca	85th	Infantry	PA	Co A
	Teamster			
Cox, John T.	25th	Infantry	NJ	Co I
Cox, William H.	35th	Infantry	NJ	Co D
Crenshaw, Aaron	1st	Cavalry	FL	Co B
Crite, Rohan	U.S.	Army	NJ	?
Croshon, Rev. David R.	141st	Infantry	OH	Co H
Crosson, Cornelius	1st	Infantry	NJ	Co A
Crosson, Thomas H.	30th	Infantry	NJ	Co C
Crowell, Jeremiah A.	2nd	Cavalry	NJ	Co M
Crowell, Jeremiah	9th	Infantry	NJ	Co K
Crowell, Joseph Edgar	13th	Infantry	NJ	Co K
Crowell, Thomas A.	9th	Infantry	NJ	Co G
Crowley, Thomas A.	4th	Infantry	NY	Co E

Cruso, Alanso	53rd	Infantry	KY	Co F
	Teamster			
Cummings, George T.	14th	Infantry	NJ	Co C
Curhary/Curhen, John	2nd	Cavalry	MD	Co D,E
	Teamster			
Dabony, Anthony	12th	Infantry	IN	Co D
	Teamster			
Daly, James	69th	Infantry	NY	Co FA
Daniels, Alva	1st	Cavalry	WI	Co H
	Teamster			
Davis, Francis	9th	Infantry	NJ	Co G
Davis, John W.	121st	Infantry	OH	Co B
Davis, Joseph H.	9th	Infantry	NJ	Co K
Davis, Luther A.	9th	Infantry	NJ	Co K
Day, Daniel	2nd	Calvalry	NJ	Co D
Day, David C.	8th	Infantry	NJ	Co B
Day, Edward I.	70th	Infantry	NY	Co K
Day, Horace H.	8th	Infantry	NY	Co F
Day, Mulford B.	15th	Infantry	NJ	Co C
Day, Samuel E.	9th	Infantry	NY	Co D
Day, William H.	8th	Infantry	NJ	Co E
De Camp, Henry W.	1st	Calvalry	NJ	Co L
De Graw, Charles R.	22nd	Infantry	NJ	Co A
De Graw, John	25th	Infantry	NY	Co K
De Hart, John W.	9th	Infantry	NJ	Co B
DeHart, William Cherwood	7th	Infantry	NY	Co F
Dener, Christian	48th	Infantry	PA	Co D
	Teamster			
Deygre, William A.	2nd	Cavalry	IN	Co C
Dhu, Dennis	91st	Infantry	NY	Co B
Dibble, William	117th	Infantry	NY	Co K
	Teamster			
Dicason, Gamalia	4th	Cavalry	MI	Co G
	Teamster			
Dickenson, Charles	6th	Infantry	NJ	Co I
Dickerson, William A.	10th	Light Art'y	NY	?

Dickson, James	52nd Infantry	IL	Co D
	Teamster		
Dishon, William A.	66th Infantry	IN	Co E
	Teamster		
Ditmars, Frederick A.	39th Infantry	NJ	Co C
Doty, Samuel K.	9th Infantry	NJ	Co G
Douglass, Robert J.	9th Infantry	NJ	Co A
Dow, Edward S.	5th Infantry	NY	Co I
Drake, George W.	15th Infantry	NJ	Co I
Drake, Henry C.	35th Infantry	NJ	Co G
Drake, Silas	14th Infantry	NJ	Co C
Drake, William H. B.	28th Infantry	NJ	Co I
Dunham, Abram	11th Infantry	NJ	Co D
Dunham, David B.	44th Infantry	NY	Co I
Dunham, Jeremiah	11th Infantry	NJ	Co D
Dunham, John B.	14th Infantry	NJ	Co E
Dunham, Randolph	11th Infantry	NJ	Co D
Dunham, Samuel	1st Infantry	NJ	Co A
Dunham, William	14th Infantry	NJ	Co D
Dunn, George	26th Infantry	NJ	Co C
Dunn, Joseph	14th Infantry	NJ	Co H
Dubois, Edward M.	14th Heavy Art'y	RI	Co B
Eaton, George	56th Infantry	MA	Co C
Ellert, Wilburn	74th Infantry	OH	Co K
Ellis, Henry C.	35th Infantry	NJ	Co E
Elson, John Henry	31st Infantry	NJ	Co K
Esterbrooks, Edward M.	44th Infantry	NY	Co B
Evans, Wilson B.	178th Infantry	OH	Co D
Evans, Wilson B.	186th Infantry	OH	?
Ezell, Davis	52nd Infantry	IL	Co D
Finch, Anthony	52nd Infantry	IL	Co E
Fisher, James	1st Light Artillery	NJ	Bat'y E
Flernay, Bateman	52nd Infantry	IL	Co E
Ford, George C.	26th Infantry	NJ	Co G
Foreman, Isaac	35th Infantry	PA	Co C
Fox, John P.	10th Heavy Art'y	NY	Co H
Francis, John C.	2nd Heavy Art''y	MA	Co I

Frank, John T.	9th	Infantry	NJ	Co H
Freeman, Charles	31st	Infantry	NJ	Co H
Freeman, Enos E.	15th	Infantry	NJ	Co G
Freeman, Eul	6th	Light Artillery	NY	Ind. Bat'y
Freeman, Thomas	9th	Infantry	NJ	Co K
Frost, Henry	10th	Infantry	NJ	Co H
Fry, Alvin	50th	Infantry	IL	Co B
Fulton, John	22nd	Infantry	NJ	Co A
Gardner, Frank	45th	Infantry	IL	Co A
Gattley, Andy	3rd	Cavalry	MA	Co F
Gerrish, Nathan	12th	Infantry	CT	Co C
Giles, James	14th	Infantry	NJ	Co C
Godfrey, William	169th	Infantry	NY	Co E
Godshalk, Samuel	104th	Infantry	PA	Co B
Goodwin, George	3rd	Infantry	NJ	Co I
Gould, George	9th	Infantry	NJ	Co C
Gould, William J.	26th	Infantry	NJ	Co F
Gracey, Abraham	52nd	Infantry	IL	Co C
Graham, Robert	9th	Infantry	NJ	Co A
Gray, Andrew	32nd	Infantry	IO	Co H
Green, Aaron	7th	Infantry	MO	Co I
Green, Samuel K.	1st	Engineers	NY	Co A
Gregory, John	28th	Infantry	NJ	Co F
Gregory, Thomas R.	15th	Infantry	NJ	Co A
Grigsby, Martin	9th	Infantry	IL	?
Grixby, Burt	9th	Infantry.	IL	?
Grunter, John	7th	Infantry	MO	Co I
Hall, Francis	1st	Infantry	NJ	Co A
Hall, George	25th	Infantry	NJ	Co D
Hall, James	13th	Infantry	NJ	Co E
Ham, James	1st	Cavalry	MO	Co H
Hand, Edward Scott	14th	Infantry	NJ	Co E
Hand, Henry Wells	136th	Infantry	NY	Co F
Hand, Jesse	14th	Infantry	NJ	Co E
Hand, John	3rd	Infantry	NJ	Co I
Hand, William	11th	Infantry	NJ	Co BI
Harvey, John H.	14th	Infantry	NJ	Co E

Name	Regiment	Branch	State	Company
Haverston, Thomas	10th	Cavalry	TN	Co B
Hawkins, Andrew	3rd	Cavalry	MA	Co F
Hedden, Jacob	8th	Infantry	NJ	Co I
Hedden, William	3rd	Infantry	NJ	Co I
Henry, Henry	162nd	Infantry	NY	Co A
Henry, John Lewis	14th	Infantry	NJ	Co C
Henry, William	14th	Infantry	NJ	Co C
Henry, Thomas	3rd	Infantry	NJ	Co D
Higgins, David S. C.	9th	Infantry	NJ	Co K
Higgins, Thomas	22nd	Infantry	NJ	Co H
High, David I.	6th	Light Artillery	NY	Ind. Bat'y
Hill, William E.	6th	Infantry	MA	Co G
Hoff, John	31st	Infantry	NJ	Co A
Holland, Abraham	30th	Infantry	NJ	Co C
Holland, George	1st	Cavalry	NJ	Co C
Holston, John M.	9th	Infantry	NJ	Co KG
Hubbard, James Frank	30th	Infantry	NJ	Co H
Hughes, Hugh	2nd	Infantry	NJ	Co A
Hughes, William H.	6th	Light Artillery	NY	Ind. Bat'y
Hunt, Jacob	30th	Infantry	NJ	Co E
Hunt, Jacob	4th	Infantry	NJ	?
Hunt, James	1st	Cavalry	NJ	Co I
Hunt, Thomas	5th	Infantry	NJ	Co A
Jackson, Abner	169th	Infantry	NY	?
	Transferred to U.S.C.T.			
Jackson, Alexander	169th	Infantry	NY	?
Jackson, Andrew	34th	Infantry	NJ	Co F
Jackson, Damion	169th	Infantry	NY	?
Jackson, John K.	9th	Infantry	NJ	Co K
Jackson, Thomas R.	3rd	Infantry	NJ	Co H
Jackson, Virgil	169th	Infantry	NY	?
Jackson, William H.	43rd	Light Artillery	PA	Co D
Jenkins, William	8th	Infantry	ME	Co G
Jerry, Davis	52nd	Infantry	IL	Co G
	Wagoner			
Jewell, Edward	8th	Infantry	NJ	Co I
Johnson, John H.	5th	Infantry	NJ	Co H

Johnson, John I.	1st	Infantry	NJ	Co I
Johnson, William H.	9th	Infantry	NJ	Co G
Johnson, William M.	9th	Infantry	NJ	Co KC
Jones, Edward	14th	Infantry	NJ	Co C
Jones, Obadiah	14th	Infantry	NJ	Co E
Jones, Williams	14th	Infantry	NJ	Co C
Jordan, Warren	52nd	Infantry	IL	E CCo
E		Wagoner		
Kane, John	9th	Infantry	NJ	Co K
Keller, Alfred	Engr., Reg't of the West		MO	Co H
Kellum, Josiah	9th	Infantry	NJ	Co K
Kennedy, Daniel	9th	Infantry	NJ	Co G
Kent, Henry C.	11th	Infantry	NJ	Co D
King, Joseph H.	9th	Infantry	NJ	Co H
Kinsey, George	30th	Infantry	NJ	Co C
Kinsey, Peter	26th	Infantry	NJ	Co A
Kinsey, William Baker	40th	Infantry	NJ	Co G
Kitchen, Moses	52nd	Infantry	IL	Co I
Kittera, James	89th	Infantry	OH	Co K
Knight, Henry	52nd	Infantry	IL	Co B
Knokwell, William	43rd	Infantry	IL	Co A
Kossurn, Kirk	52nd	Infantry	IL	Co C
Lamb, James	52nd	Infantry	IL	Co A
Lamb, William	123rd	Infantry	NY	?
Layton, Samuel	2nd	Cavalry	NJ	Co M
Leachman, John	40th	Infantry	IL	Co D
Lee, Peter	2nd	Cavalry	NJ	Co D
Leeds, Henry H.	6th	Cavalry	PA	?
Leonard, Charles	6th	Light Artillery	NY	Ind. Bat'y
Lincoln, Charles	52nd	Infantry	IL	Co H
Littell, William	3rd	Infantry	NJ	Co G
Little, Henry	29th	Infantry	NJ	Co F
Little, Isaac	9th	Infantry	NJ	Co F
Little, Jacob	14th	Infantry	NJ	Co E
Little, James	14th	Infantry	NJ	Co E
Loach, John	17th	Infantry	?	?
Long, John W.	14th	Infantry	NJ	Co E
Long, William	9th	Infantry	NJ	Co C

Love, Marshall	39th	Infantry	NJ	Co K
Lymus, Brayden	50th	Infantry	IL	Co H
Mahoney, Daniel	13th	Infantry	ME	Co B
Malone, Willis	52nd	Infantry	IL	Co B
Manning, William Henry	123rd	Infantry	NJ	Co A
Marsh, Charles	39th	Infantry	NJ	Co G
Marsh, Clarence W.	8th	Infantry	MA	Co A
Marsh, Edwin	6th	Light Artillery	NY Ind. Bat'y	
Marsh, Ellis	6th	Light Artillery	NY Ind. Bat'y	
Marsh, Joseph N.	14th	Infantry	NJ	Co E
Marsh, Randolph	2nd	Infantry	NJ	Co C
Marsh, Robert	20th	Infantry	MA	Co D
Marsh, Silas	30th	Infantry	NJ	Co C
Marsh, Solomon H.	8th	Infantry	NJ	Co I
Marsh, Stephen	40th	Infantry	NJ	Co C
Marsh, William G.	30th	Infantry	NJ	Co C
Marsh, William R.	14th	Infantry	NJ	Co E
Marshall, Charles	46th	Infantry	IL	Co E
Martin, John V.	14th	Infantry	NJ	Co C
Martin, John W.	6th	Light Artillery	NY Ind. Bat'y	
Martin, Joseph W.	6th	Light Artillery	NY Ind. Bat'y	
Maxwell, Henry T.	9th	Infantry	NJ	Co K
Maybry, John	49th	Infantry	IL	Co D
McCrossen, Thomas H.	6th	Light Artillery	NY Ind. Bat'y	
McDade, James	4th	Cavalry	WI	Co F
McDonald, John	9th	Infantry	NJ	Co G
McDonald, John	12th	Cavalry	PA	Co F
McDonald, John	6th	Light Artillery	NY Ind. Bat'y	
Mcfarland, Henry	8th	Infantry	NJ	Co I
Miller, Cornelius	6th	Light Artillery	NY Ind. Bat'y	
Miller, Debrix	4th	Infantry	MI	Co F
Miller, John I.	5th	Infantry	NJ	Co H
Miller, John V.	1st	Infantry	NJ	Co A
Morris, Cornelius	177th	Infantry	NY	Co B
Morse, Joseph E.	39th	Infantry	NJ	Co K
Morse, William	3rd	Cavalry	NJ	Co F
Mulford, Isaac	3rd	Cavalry	NJ	Co A

Mulford, John K.	10th	Infantry	NJ	Co B
Mulligan, Charles	26th	Infantry	NJ	Co E
Murray, John F.	9th	Infantry	NJ	Co K
Murray, Samuel	9th	Infantry	NJ	Co G
Murray, Thomas	11th	Infantry	NJ	Co R
Murry, William	18th	Infantry	NY	Co D
Neill, Stephen	?	Infantry	IL	?
Nelson, James H. C.	26th	Infantry	NJ	Co C
Newbern, William H.	9th	Infantry	NJ	Co K A
Nickerson, George	92nd	Infantry	IL	Co E
Noe, Dallas	2nd	Cavalry	NJ	Co A
Noe, Elmer	14th	Infantry	NJ	Co E
Noe, Smith H.	5th	Infantry	NJ	Co H
Norman, William	36th	Infantry	IN	Co I
Nun, Henry	9th	Infantry	NJ	Co G
Oliver, George	52nd	Infantry	IL	Co B
Oliver, Jeremiah	1st	Infantry	NJ	Co B
Olmstead, William H.	2nd	Heavy Art'y	NY	Co H
Owen, Isaac	52nd	Infantry	IL	Co I
Owens, Oliver	52nd	Infantry	IL	Co C
Parham, John	6th	Infantry	MO	Co B
Parker, Edward	23rd	Infantry	NJ	Co G
Parker, James E.	9th	Heavy Art'y	NY	Co B
Parker, John	9th	Infantry	NJ	Co K
Pate, Henry	50th	Infantry	IL	Co F
Patterson, William	28th	Infantry	NJ	Co F
Payton, Philip	72nd	Infantry	IN	Co G
Peach, Frederick G.	9th	Infantry	NJ	Co G
Peacock, John	9th	Infantry	NJ	Co K
Peer/Pur, Tunis	9th	Infantry	NJ`	Co K
Pender, Pattie	46th	Infantry	OH	?
Pennington, Nathan	28th	Infantry	NJ	Co C
Perkins, John	34th	Infantry	NJ	Co D
Pernell, Jacob	91st	Infantry	NY	Co B
Perry, Jerry	187th	Infantry	NY	Co K
Phillips, James P.	8th	Infantry	NJ	Co I
Plum, George M., Jr.	6th	Light Artillery	NY	Ind. Bat'y

Post, Jacob	22nd	Infantry	NJ	Co A
Potter, David	14th	Infantry	NJ	Co E
Potter, Edward C.	173rd	Infantry	NY	Co C
Potter, George N.	2nd	Infantry	NJ	Co A
Potter, George	117th	Infantry	NY	Co G
Potter, Henry L.	7th	Infantry	NJ	Co K
Potter, John	14th	Infantry	NJ	Co KF
Potter, John W.	6th	Light Artillery	NY	Ind. Bat'y
Potter, Joseph M.	6th	Light Artillery	NY	Ind. Bat'y
Potter, William E.	12th	Infantry	NJ	Co K, G
Powell, William H.	1st	Cavalry	NJ	Co A
Powers, John S.	11th	Infantry	NJ	Co B
Price, John E.	9th	Infantry	NJ	Co K
Price, John H.	3rd	Infantry	NJ	Co K
Provost, William W.	134th	Infantry	NY	
	Unassigned			
Quinn, James	8th	Infantry	NJ	Co H
Rae, Augustus	11th	Infantry	NJ	Co H
Ramsey, Abraham	59th	Infantry	IL	Co K
Ramsey, William	96th	Infantry	PA	?
Randolph, Charles H.	30th	Infantry	NJ	Co H
Randolph, James F.	70th	Infantry	NY	Co D
Randolph, Joseph C.	30th	Infantry	NJ	Co H
Randolph, Theodore	6th	Light Artillery	NY	Ind. Bat'y
Randolph, William B.	12th	Light Art'y	NY	?
Randolph, William B.	1st	Light Artillery	NJ	Co B
Randolph, William H.	6th	Infantry	NJ	Co K
Ray, John H.	43rd	Infantry	NY	Co I
Reed, David	9th	Infantry	NJ	Co KG
Reeder, James	1st	Light Artillery	RI	Co G
Reese, Samuel W.	1st	Cavalry	PA	Co G
Reynolds, Ashley	132nd	Infantry	NY	Co H
Reynolds, Ashley	99th	Infantry	NY	Co B
Richardson, Samuel	4th	Infantry	MI	Co E
Rickets, John W.	9th	Infantry	NJ	Co K
Riley, James	9th	Infantry	NJ	Co G
Riley, Michael	1st	Artillery	NJ	Bat'y B

Rivers, Preston	52nd	Infantry	IL	Co A
Roberts, Samuel L.	15th	Infantry	NJ	Co K
Roberts, Thomas	52nd	Infantry	IL	Co B
Robeson, Philip	55th	Infantry	PA	Co H
Robeson, Toby	55th	Infantry	PA	Co H
Robinson, John Howard	7th	Infantry	NJ	Co G
Robinson, Rufus	121st	Infantry	NY	Co D
Robinson, Samuel I.	11th	Infantry	NJ	Co E
Robinson, Thomas Peter	6th	Infantry	NJ	Co H
Roll, John K.	52nd	Infantry	NY	Co C
Ropes, Elihu H.	11th	Ind. Bat'y	NY	?
Rose, Henry T.	14th	Infantry	NJ	Co E
Rose, Royal H.	30th	Infantry	NJ	Co H
Ross, James	15th	Infantry	NJ	Co B
Ross, Joseph		Infantry	U.S. Army	
Ryan, John R. T.	4th	Infantry	NJ	Co A
Ryno, John	14th	Infantry	NJ	Co E
Ryno, William	2nd	Infantry	NJ	Co D
Sanders, Jonathan B.	50th	Infantry	NY	Co F
Sax, Henry	5th	Infantry	NJ	Co H
Schenck, John Henry	70th	Infantry	NY	Co D
Schenk, Henry F.	9th	Infantry	NJ	Co E
Schenk, Peter	15th	Infantry	NJ	Co E
Scott, Charles H.	24th	Infantry	NJ	Co I
Scott, Martin	19th	Infantry	IN	?
Scott, William A.	1st	Infantry	NJ	Co A
Simmonds, John W.	9th	Infantry	NJ	Co K
Simmons, Ned	155th	Infantry	NY	Co D
Simmons, Thomas S.	84th	Infantry	NY	Co B
Simmons, William	52nd	Infantry	IL	Co I
Simms, John W.	6th Light Artillery		NY Ind. Bat'y	
Simms, William H.	1st	Engineers	MI	Co I
Simpson, Benjamin	52nd	Infantry	IL	Co G
Slater, Edward	14th	Infantry	NJ	Co C
Slater, Samuel	30th	Infantry	NJ	Co H
Smart. Elick	8th	Infantry	ME	Co C
Smith, Alexander	46th	Infantry	IL	Co F

Smith, George	9th	Infantry	NJ	Co G
Smith, Henry	46th	Infantry	IL	Co E
Smith, Jack	52nd	Infantry	IL	Co I
Smith, James	9th	Infantry	NJ	Co K
Smith, John W. B.	11th	Infantry	NJ	Co B
Smith, Sandy	10	Infantry	OH	Co K
Smith, William M.	9th	Infantry	NJ	Co G
Solomon, David	52nd	Infantry	IL	Co E
Springer, George	50th	Infantry	IL	Co B
Springfield, Reuben	52nd	Infantry	IL	Co I
Stagner, Barclay	8th	Cavalry	PA	Co M
Stanford, Henry	101st	Infantry	NY	Co A
Stansbury, Joseph S.	1st	Infantry	NJ	Co G
Starks, Henry	8th	Infantry	MO	Co H
Steele, Green	Unassigned		IL	?
Steeley, Caleb	8th	Infantry	MI	Co F
Stephenson, John W.	2nd	Infantry	NH	Co G
Steward, Stephen	7th	Cavalry	PA	Co K
Stewart, John E.	44th	Infantry	NY	Co D
Stewart, William Scott	83rd	Infantry	PA	?
Stewart, William Scott	40th	Infantry	NJ	Co D
Still, Charles R.	82nd	Infantry	NY	Co k
Stokes, Henry	46th	Infantry	IL	Co F
Strander, Erren	69th	Infantry	OH	?
Sutton, Aaron	11th	Infantry	NJ	Co B
Sutton, Benjamin	67th	Infantry	NY	Co H
Sutton, Charles	14th	Infantry	NJ	Co D
Sutton, Peter	52nd	Infantry	IL	Co I
Sykes, Abraham	8th	Infantry	ME	Co C
Taylor, Charles H.	8th	Infantry	NJ	Co I
	Teamster			
Terhune, Cornelius	23rd	Infantry	NJ	Co H
Terhune, David W.	22nd	Infantry	NJ	Co C
Terhune, John W.	11th	Infantry	NJ	Co D
Terhune, Martin	22nd	Infantry	NJ	Co A
Thomas, Calvin	161	Infantry	NY	Co A
Thompson, Rev. Thomas	9th	Infantry	NJ	Co G

Thompson, William	3rd Cavalry	MI	Co K
Thorn, Randolph	30th Infantry	NJ	Co H
Thorn, Thompson	6th Light Artillery	NY	Ind. Bat'y
Thornton, George	2nd Cavalry	NJ	Co F
Tichnor, Jacob	2nd Cavalry	MO	?
Tidwell, John	Unassigned	IL	?
Tidwell, Thornton	Unassigned	IL	?
Till, Samuel M.	13th Infantry	NJ	Co K
Tilton, Henry	11th Infantry	NJ	Co B
Tooker, Nathan	2nd Infantry	NJ	Co A
Turner, Samuel	13th Infantry	NJ	Co B
Turnville, Charles	8th Infantry	MO	Co F
Tuttle, George	27th Infantry	NJ	Co E
Van Campen, Eugene	1st Heavy Art'y	NY	Co A
Van Horn, John W.	14th Infantry	NJ	Co A
Van Horn, William H.	2nd Infantry	NJ	Co A
Van Houten, James C.	14th Infantry	NJ	Co C
Van Houton, John J.	22nd Infantry	NJ	Co A
Van Pelt, David H.	11th Infantry	NJ	Co B
Van Pelt, George	4th Heavy Art'y	NY	Co E
Van Pelt, Jacob D.	11th Infantry	NJ	Co B
Van Pelt, Jeremiah	11th Infantry	NJ	Co B
Van Riper, John	27th Infantry	NJ	Co G
Van Sickles, Albert	14th Infantry	NJ	Co E
Vanderhoven, Jessie	30th Infantry	NJ	Co C
Vanderveer, Peter	70th Infantry	NJ	Co K
Vanderveer, William H.	32nd Infantry	NY	Co G
Vannaman, William	30th Infantry	NJ	Co C
VanVactor, John	2nd Cavalry	MO	Co A
Vermeule, Nathan P.	30th Infantry	NJ	Co H
Victor, Ela	133rd Infantry	NY	Co F
Voorhees, Charles A.	11th Infantry	NJ	Co B
Voorhees, Edmund A.	14th Infantry	NJ	Co C
Voorhees, Henry	9th Infantry	NJ	Co C
Voorhees, Jeremiah	11th Infantry	NY	Co B
Voorhees, Jeremiah F.	9th Infantry	NY	Co A
Voorhees, John C.	11th Infantry	NJ	Co B

Voorhis, Nicholas	22nd	Infantry	NJ	Co A
Walker, Thomas	14th	Infantry	NJ	Co C
Wallace, John	13th	Infantry	NJ	Co K
Ward, Charles	9th	Infantry	NJ	Co G
Ward, Frank	3rd	Cavalry	MA	Co C
Ward, John	9th	Infantry	NJ	Co K
Ward, Thomas	14th	Infantry	NJ	Co E
Ward, William	9th	Infantry	NJ	Co G
Warren, Allen	52nd	Infantry	IL	Co K
Warren, George	52nd	Infantry	IL	Co H
Warren, Samuel	52nd	Infantry	IL	
	Unassigned			
Washington, Williams	51st	Infantry	NY	Co E
Watson, George	3rd	Infantry	NJ	Co K
Watson, Pope	78th	Infantry	IL	Co I
Watson, Thomas	14th	Infantry	NJ	Co I
Webster, York	14th	Cavalry	NY	Co C
Weeks, Thomas	31st	Infantry	WI	Co A
White, Alexander	52nd	Infantry	IL	Co G
White, Charles	45th	Infantry	IL	Co A
White, Charles	9th	Militia	NY	Co K
White, George	14th	Infantry	NJ	Co G
White, James	35th	Infantry	NJ	Co H
White, Louis	14th	Heavy Art'y	ny	Co H
Whitehead, George	9th	Infantry	NJ	CoK
Whitehead, James	13th	Infantry	NJ	Co K
Whitney, George	9th	Infantry	NJ	Co G
Williams, Aaron	137th	Infantry	IL	Co C
Williams, Charles	52nd	Infantry	IL	Co H
Williams, Charles	9th	Infantry	NJ	Co K
Williams, Edward	132	Infantry	NY	Co H
Williams, Frederick	38th	Infantry	NJ	Co K
Williams, George	49th	Infantry	IL	Co D
Williams, James H.	9th	Infantry	NJ	Co G
Williams, Robert S.	9th	Infantry	NJ	Co K
Williams, William H.	9th	Infantry	NJ	Co A

Willis, Malone	52nd	Infantry	IL	Co C
	Wagoner			
Wills, William H.	24th	Infantry	NJ	Co B
Wilson, Andrew	159th	Infantry	NY	Co H
Wilson, Henry F.	14th	Infantry	NJ	Co C
Wilson, Henry	2nd	Infantry	NJ	Co A
Wilson, James	5th	Infantry	NJ	Co H
Wilson, Lafayette	52nd	Infantry	IL	Co K
Winans, Alfred L.	11th	Infantry	NJ	Co D
Winans, Theodore	13th	Infantry	NJ	Co B
Wolfe, Andrew	52nd	Infantry	IL	Co F
Wood, Amos	29th	Infantry	NJ	Co F
Wood, Henry	10th	Infantry	NJ	Co I
Woods, Charles	3rd	Infantry	NJ	Co K
Woods, Henry	Nield's Indpt. Battery		DE	Art'y
Wright, Edward	21st	Infantry	NJ	Co H
Wright, James	3rd	Infantry	NJ	Co C
Wyckoff, Benjamin	31st	Infantry	NJ	Co A
Wyckoff, Charles	48th	Infantry	NY	Co HA
Zabriske, Jacob H.	114th	Infantry	NY	Co D

ADDITIONAL BLACK SOLDIERS BY STATES

CALIFORNIA

Callaghan, Michael F.	2nd Farrier	Cavalry	CA	Co M

CONNECTICUT

Gerrish, Nathan	12th	Infantry	CT	Co C

DELAWARE

Woods, Henry	Nield's Indpt. Battery	DE	Art'y

FLORIDA

Crenshaw, Aaron	1st	Cavalry	FL	Co B

ILLINOIS

Adams, Anson	108th Wagoner	Infanty	IL	Co G
Adkins, Jacob	52nd Teamster	Infantry	IL	Co F
Allen, Wallace	66th	Infantry	IL	Co K
Anderson, Nathan	52nd	Infantry	IL	Co K
Archy, Torian	42nd	Infantry	IL	Co K
Armstead, Willis	52nd	Infantry	IL	Co D
Atskuson, Robert	12th Saddler	Cavalry	IL	Co C
Babbett, John C.	11th Saddler	Cavalry	IL	Co. F

Barrett, Daniel	1st	Cavalry	IL	Co C
	Blacksmith/Farrier			
Beath, Edward	5th	Cavalry	IL	Co C
	Saddler			
Berlew, Jonathan	116th	Infantry	IL	Co H
	Teamster			
Biggers, Aaron	52nd	Infantry	IL	Co I
Blackson, James C.	11th	Cavalry	IL	Co C
	Saddler			
Bolen, Benjamin	85th	Infantry	IL	Co H
	Teamster			
Borkhous, William	2nd	Cavalry	IL	Co G
	Saddler			
Bown, Henry	52nd	Infantry	IL	Co G
Braden, Porter	50th	Infantry	IL	Co D
Brown, Joe	43rd	Infantry	IL	Co K
Brown, John	50th	Infantry	IL	Co K
Brown, William D.	81st	Infantry	IL	Co G
	Teamster			
Bucknells, James	115th	Infantry	IL	Co D
	Teamster			
Brusweller, Harrison	10th	Cavalry	IL	Co A
	Saddler			
Buck, Julius	10th	Cavalry	IL	Co CA
	Saddler			
Clark, Felix	87th	Infantry	IL	Co K
	Teamster			
Clinger/Clingle, John	66th	Infantry	IL	Co E,B
	Teamster			
Collins, John	98th	Infantry	IL	Co E
	Teamster			
Conour, John	60th	Infantry	IL	Co F
	Teamster			
Dickson, James	52nd	Infantry	IL	Co D
	Teamster			
Ezell, Davis	52nd	Infantry	IL	Co D

Finch, Anthony	52nd	Infantry	IL	Co E
Flernay, Bateman	52nd	Infantry	IL	Co E
Fry, Alvin	50th	Infantry	IL	Co B
Gardner, Frank	45th	Infantry	IL	Co A
Gracey, Abraham	52nd	Infantry	IL	Co C
Grigsby, Martin	9th	Infantry	IL	?
Grixby, Burt	9th	Infantry.	IL	?
Jerry, Davis	52nd	Infantry	IL	Co G
	Wagoner			
Jordan, Warren	52nd	Infantry	IL	Co E
	Wagoner			
Kitchen, Moses	52nd	Infantry	IL	Co I
Knight, Henry	52nd	Infantry	IL	Co B
Knokwell, William	43rd	Infantry	IL	Co A
Kossurn, Kirk	52nd	Infantry	IL	Co C
Lamb, James	52nd	Infantry	IL	Co A
Leachman, John	40th	Infantry	IL	Co D
Lincoln, Charles	52nd	Infantry	IL	Co H
Lymus, Brayden	50th	Infantry	IL	Co H
Malone, Willis	52nd	Infantry	IL	Co B
Marshall, Charles	46th	Infantry	IL	Co E
Maybry, John	49th	Infantry	IL	Co D
Neill, Stephen	?	Infantry	IL	?
Nickerson, George	92nd	Infantry	IL	Co E
Oliver, George	52nd	Infantry	IL	Co B
Owen, Isaac	52nd	Infantry	IL	Co I
Owens, Oliver	52nd	Infantry	IL	Co C
Pate, Henry	50th	Infantry	IL	Co F
Ramsey, Abraham	59th	Infantry	IL	Co K
Rivers, Preston	52nd	Infantry	IL	Co A
Roberts, Thomas	52nd	Infantry	IL	Co B
Simmons,William	52nd	Infantry	IL	Co I
Simpson, Benjamin	52nd	Infantry	IL	Co G
Smith, Alexander	46th	Infantry	IL	Co F
Smith, Henry	46th	Infantry	IL	Co E
Smith, Jack	52nd	Infantry	IL	Co I
Solomon, David	52nd	Infantry	IL	Co E

Springer, George	50th	Infantry	IL	Co B
Springfield, Reuben	52nd	Infantry	IL	Co I
Steele, Green	Unassigned		IL	
Stokes, Henry	46th	Infantry	IL	Co F
Sutton, Peter	52nd	Infantry	IL	Co I
Tidwell, John	Unassigned		IL	
Tidwell, Thornton	Unassigned		IL	
Warren, Allen	52nd	Infantry	IL	Co K
Warren, George	52nd	Infantry	IL	Co H
Warren, Samuel	52nd	Infantry	IL	?
	Unassigned			
Watson, Pope	78th	Infantry	IL	Co I
White, Alexander	52nd	Infantry	IL	Co G
White, Charles	45th	Infantry	IL	Co A
Williams, Aaron	137th	Infantry	IL	Co C
Williams, Charles	52nd	Infantry	IL	Co H
Williams, George	49th	Infantry	IL	Co D
Willis, Malone	52nd	Infantry	IL	Co C
	Wagoner			
Wilson, Lafayette	52nd	Infantry	IL	Co K
Wolfe, Andrew	52nd	Infantry	IL	Co F

INDIANA

Abbott, William	100th	Infantry	IN	Co B
	Teamster			
Abner, John	75th	Infantry	IN	Co C
	Teamster			
Acoam, John W.	4th	Cavalry	IN	Co G
	Saddler			
Acuff, John T.	1st	Cavalry	IN	Co H
	Blacksmith/Farrier			
Adams, David O.	4th	Cavalry	IN	Co A
	Teamster			
Allen, William T.	84th	Infantry	IN	Co K
	Teamster			

Name	Unit	Branch	State	Company
Anderson, Reason T.	13th	Cavalry	IN	Co I
	Saddler			
Atkinson, William	11th	Cavalry	IN	Co D
	Saddler			
Baits, Abraham	58th	Infantry	IN	Co E
	Teamster			
Ballsover, Alfred	1st	Cavalry	IN	Co B
	Saddler			
Barber, Peter	114th	Infantry	IN	Co I
	Teamster			
Barbra/Barlrey/Peter	144th	Infantry	IN	Co I
	Teamster			
Bayless, Platt	11th	Cava;ry	IN	Co H
	Teamster			
Bayly, Dock L.	4th	Cavalry	IN	Co E
	Teamster			
Beam/Beans, Aaron	49TH	Infantry	IN	Co B
Bearach, William	23rd	Infantry	IN	Co A
	Teamster			
Beezely/Beezly, Nathaniel	2nd	Cavalry	IN	Co B
	Farrier			
Berlew, Jonathan	116th	Infantry	IL	Co H
	Teamster			
Carr, Berry	22nd	Infantry	IN	Co G
Carr, Jacob	82nd	Infantry	IN	Co F
Birt, Andrew	3rd	Cavalry	IN	Co L
	Teamster			
Bishop, Cleveland	7th	Cavalry	IN	Co AC
	Saddler			
Bowan, James	7th	Cavalry	IN	Co E
	Saddler			
Bulsover, Alfred	1st	Cavalry	IN	Co B
	Saddler			
Bumgardner, Jefferson	9th	Cavalry	IN	Co KA
	Teamster			
Buris, Charles	80th	Infantry	IN	Co B
	Teamster			

Clines, Jacob	137th	Infantry	IN	Co I
	Teamster			
Dabony, Anthony	12th	Infantry	IN	Co D
	Teamster			
Dishon, William A.	66th	Infantry	IN	Co E
	Teamster			
Douglas, William	66th	Infantry	IN	Co C
Dabony, Anthony	12th	Infantry	IN	Co D
	Teamster			
Norman, William	36th	Infantry	IN	Co I
Payton, Philip	72nd	Infantry	IN	Co G
Scott, Martin	19th	Infantry	IN	?

IOWA

Bailey, John A.	1st	Cavary	IO	Co K
	Saddler			
Beh, Benedict	6th	Cavalry	IO	Co H,F
	Saddler			
Birkhall, Francis P.	1st	Cavalry	IO	Co H
	Farrier			
Gray, Andrew	32nd	Infantry	IO	Co H
Loach, John	17th	Infantry	IO	?

KANSAS

Ables, Henry	15th	Cavalry	KS	Co L
	Bugler			
Briant, William C.	7th	Cavalry	KS	Co H
	Saddler			
Babbitt, James	6th	Cavalry	KS	Co A,E
	Saddler			
Barnett, James B.	16th	Cavalry	KS	Co C,I
	Farrier			

KENTUCKY

Atkinson, John R.	3rd	Cavalry	KY	Co A
	Blacksmith/Farrier			
Baker, James H.	14th	Cavalry	KY	Co G
	Saddler			
Beam, Jesse L.	15th	Cavalry	KY	Co A
	Teamster			
Becknell, William H.	14th	Cavalry	KY	Co F
	Teamster			
Begley, Asa	14th	Cavalry	KY	Co M
	Teamster			
Boots, Jacob	9th	Cavalry	KY	Co C
	Farrier			
Burns, James J.	6th	Cavalry	KY	Co G
	Saddler			
Burton, David	12th	Cavalry	KY	Co LEC
	Teamster			
Cherry, John	12th	Cavalry	KY	Co F
	Teamster			
Coslow, Marion	4th	Infantry	KY	Co F
	Teamster		Mounted	
Cruso, Alanso	53rd	Infantry	KY	Co F
	Teamster			

MAINE

Jenkins, William	8th	Infantry	ME	Co G
Mahoney, Daniel	13th	Infantry	ME	Co B
Smart. Elick	8th	Infantry	ME	Co C
Sykes, Abraham	8th	Infantry	ME	

MARYLAND

Cakarice, Michael	1st	Cavalry	MD	Co B
	Farrier			
Cosgrove, William	Smith's Ind'pt	Cavalry	MD	?
	Teamster			

Curhary/Curhen, John	2nd	Cavalry	MD	Co D,E
	Teamster			

MASSACHUSETTS

Chamberlain, Edmond D.	51st	Infantry	MA	Co E B
Chamberlain, Wm. Conner	23rd	Infantry	MA	Co D
Eaton, George	56th	Infantry	MA	Co C
Francis, John C.	2nd	Heavy Art'y	MA	I
Gattley, Andy	3rd	Cavalry	MA	Co F
Hawkins, Andrew	3rd	Cavalry	MA	Co F
Hill, William E.	6th	Infantry	MA	Co G
	15th	Light Art'y	MA	?
	6th	Light Art'y	MA	?
Marsh, Clarence W.	8th	Infantry	MA	Co A
Marsh, Robert	20th	Infantry	MA	Co D
Ward, Frank	3rd	Cavalry	MA	Co C

MICHIGAN

Abbott, Silas	2nd	Infantry	MI	Co G
	Teamster			
Ackles, William	2nd	Militia Cav.	MI	Co E
	Saddler			
Aldrich, Joel	6th	Cavalry	MI	Co M
	Teamster			
Alton/Alten, Henry	4th	Cavalry	MI	Co F
	Teamster			
Ambrooke, Charles	2nd	Cavalry	MI	Co K
	Saddler			
Armfield, Herk	19th	Infantry	MI	Co K
	Teamster			
Atterbery, Isaac T.	1st	Cavalry	MO	Co L
	Saddler			
Auble, James	6th	Cavalry	MI	Co A
	Teamster			

Babcock, William F.	4th	Cavalry	MI	Co E
	Teamster			
Backhouse, Hermann	3rd	Cavalry	MI	Co E
	Teamster			
Baker, George	7th	Cavalry	MI	Co B
	Teamster			
Baldwin, Byron	27th	Infantry	MI	Co A
	Teamster			
Baldwin, George	4th	Infantry	MI	Co K
	Teamster			
Balleu, Banjamin	3rd	Cavalry	MO	Co CBD
	Farrier			
Ballinger, James	5th	Cavalry	MI	Co D
	Teamster			
Barrows, William P.	5th	Cavalry	MI	Co L
	Farrier			
Baurs, Jacob	4th	Cavalry	MI	Co D
	Teamster			
Beckwith, John	8th	Infantry	MI	Co C
	Teamster			
Bennett, George H.	10th	Cavalry	MI	Co K
	Farrier			
Buman/Beeman, Joel S.	2nd	Cavalry	MI	Co F
	Saddler			
Cary, Anson	6th	Cavalry	MI	Co M
	Teamster			
Cary, Hiram	8th	Cavalry	MI	Co M
	Teamster			
Dicason, Gamalia	4th	Cavalry	MI	Co G
	Teamster			
Miller, Debrix	4th	Infantry	MI	Co F
Richardson, Samuel	4th	Infantry	MI	Co E
Simms, William H.	1st	Engineers	MI	Co I
Steeley, Caleb	8th	Infantry	MI	Co F
Thompson, William	3rd	Cavalry	MI	Co K

MISSOURI

Name	Regiment		State	Company
Arthur, William H.	10th	Cavalry	MO	Co A
	Blacksmith/Farrier			
Atterbery, Isaac T.	1st	Cavalry	MO	Co L
	Saddler			
Berg, Adam	5th	Cavalry	MO	Co A
	Farrier			
Beirtling, Charles	7th	Cavalry	MO	Co F,A
	Saddler		S.M	
Bonebright/Bonebrite, Jacob	7th	Cavalry	MO	Co M
	Farrier			
Breysacher, John	1st	Cavalry	MO	Co KC
	Saddler			
Calvin, George W.	3rd	Cavalry	MO	Co F
	Farrier			
Calvin, Horace	10th	Cavalry	MO	Co. C
	Farrier			
Green, Aaron	7th	Infantry	MO	Co I
Grunter, John	7th	Infantry	MO	Co I
Ham, James	1st	Cavalry	MO	Co H
Keller, Alfred	Engr., Reg't of the West		MO	Co H
Parham, John	6th	Infantry	MO	Co B
Rivers, Thomas	8th	Infantry	MO	Co C
Starks, Henry	8th	Infantry	MO	Co H
Tichnor, Jacob	2nd	Cavalry	MO	?
Turnville, Charles	8th	Infantry	MO	Co F
	Teamster			
VanVactor, John	2nd	Cavalry	MO	Co A

NEBRASKA TERRITORY

Name	Regiment		State	Company
Allen, Samuel	2nd	Cavalry	NE	Co D
	Saddler			
Case, Daniel W.	2nd	Cavalry	NE	Co A
	Teamster			

NEW HAMPSHIRE

Stephenson, John W.	2nd	Infantry	NH	Co G

NEW JERSEY

Ackerman, Phillip	7th	Infantry	NJ	Co E
Ackerman, William	22nd	Infantry	NJ	Co A
Adams, Charles	14th	Infantry	NJ	Co C
Alan, Christopher	26th	Infantry	NJ	Co A
Anderson, John	9th	Infantry	NJ	Co A
Anderson, Stewart	2nd	Infantry	NJ	Co D
Anderson, Thomas	3rd	Infantry	NJ	Co A
Anthony, Henry	11th	Infantry	NJ	Co B
Ash, George W.	9th	Infantry	NJ	Co K
Ash, Henry	3rd	Infantry	NJ	Co K
Avery, George B.	1st	Artillary	NJ	Bat'yD
Avery, Thomas	4th	Infantry	NJ	Co B
Avery, William	30th	Infantry	NJ	Co C
Baker, Aaron	38th	Infantry	NJ	Co G
Baker, John	26th	Infantry	NJ	Co K
Baker, William	5th	Infantry	NJ	Co F
Baldwin, Edward	9th	Infantry	NJ	Co K
Baldwin, John	14th	Infantry	NJ	Co I
Bauer, George	1st	Cavalry	NJ	Co C
Bennett, John R.	22nd	Infantry	NJ	Co A
Benson, Charles	34th	Infantry	NJ	Co A
Brill, George W.	8th	Infantry	NJ	Co I
Brinkerhoff, George A.	22nd	Infantry	NJ	Co A
Brinkerhoff, John D.	22nd	Infantry	NJ	Recruit
Brokaw, Edwin	37th	Infantry	NJ	Co C
Brokaw, Isaac I.	3rd	Infantry	NJ	Co I
Brown, Alexander	11th	Infantry	NJ	Co D
Brown, Charles M.	9th	Infantry	NJ	Co K
Brown, Henry	9th	Infantry	NJ	Co C
Carman, Daniel V.	5th	Infantry	NJ	Co H
Champion, John G.	12th	Infantry	NJ	Co I

Chew, William H.	9th	Infantry	NJ	Co K
Clark, Isaac	3rd	Infantry	NJ	Co A
Clark, John R.	22nd	Infantry	NJ	Co A
Clark, Robert	8th	Infantry	NJ	Co I
Clark, Thomas	14th	Infantry	NJ	Co E
Cochrane, William H.	33rd	Infantry	NJ	Co K
Connett, Johnathan T.	30th	Infantry	NJ	Co H
Connelly, Michael	9th	Infantry	NJ	Co G
Conover, Jacob	9th	Infantry	NJ	Co G
Conover, Samuel	28th	Infantry	NJ	Co C
Conroy, John	9th	Infantry	NJ	Co K
Cook, Alfred	9th	Infantry	NJ	Co B
Cook, Charles	9th	Infantry	NJ	Co A
Cook, James	9th	Infantry	NJ	Co K
Cook, Peter	11th	Infantry	NJ	Co B
Cook, William	1st	Cavalry	NJ	Co C
Cooley, James	3rd	Cavalry	NJ	Co F
Corcoran, John	9th	Infantry	NJ	Co K
Cox, John T.	25th	Infantry	NJ	Co I
Cox, William H.	35th	Infantry	NJ	Co D
Crosson, Cornelius	1st	Infantry	NJ	Co A
Crosson, Thomas H.	30th	Infantry	NJ	Co C
Crowell, Jeremiah	9th	Infantry	NJ	Co K
Crowell, Joseph Edgar	13th	Infantry	NJ	Co K
Crowell, Jeremiah A.	2nd	Calvalry	NJ	Co M
Crowell, Thomas A.	9th	Infantry	NJ	Co G
Cummings, George T.	14th	Infantry	NJ	Co C
Davis, Francis	9th	Infantry	NJ	Co G
Davis, Joseph H.	9th	Infantry	NJ	Co K
Davis, Luther A.	9th	Infantry	NJ	Co K
Day, Daniel	2nd	Calvalry	NJ	Co D
Day, David C.	8th	Infantry	NJ	Co B
Day, Horace H.	8th	Infantry	NJ	Co F
Day, Mulford B.	15th	Infantry	NJ	Co C
Day, Samuel E.	9th	Infantry	NJ	Co D
Day, William H.	8th	Infantry	NJ	Co E
De Camp, Henry W.	1st	Calvalry	NJ	Co L

De Graw, Charles R.	22nd	Infantry	NJ	Co A
De Graw, John	25th	Infantry	NJ	Co K
De Hart, John W.	9th	Infantry	NJ	Co B
Dickenson, Charles	6th	Infantry	NJ	Co I
Ditmars, Frederick A.	39th	Infantry	NJ	Co C
Doty, Samuel K.	9th	Infantry	NJ	Co G
Douglass, Robert J.	9th	Infantry	NJ	Co A
Drake, George W.	15th	Infantry	NJ	Co I
Drake, Henry C.	35th	Infantry	NJ	Co G
Drake, Silas	14th	Infantry	NJ	Co C
Drake, William H. B.	28th	Infantry	NJ	Co I
	1st	Artillery	NJ	Bat'y D
Dunham, Abram	11th	Infantry	NJ	Co D
Dunham, Enoch	15th	Infantry	US Army	Co G
Dunham, Jeremiah	11th	Infantry	NJ	Co D
Dunham, John B.	14th	Infantry	NJ	Co E
Dunham, Randolph	11th	Infantry	NJ	Co D
Dunham, Samuel	1st	Infantry	NJ	Co A
Dunham, William	14th	Infantry	NJ	Co D
Dunn, George	26th	Infantry	NJ	Co C
Dunn, Joseph	14th	Infantry	NJ	Co H
Ellis, Henry C.	35th	Infantry	NJ	Co E
Elson, John Henry	31st	Infantry	NJ	Co K
Fisher, James	1st	Light Artillery	NJ	Bat'y E
Ford, George C.	26th	Infantry	NJ	Co G
Frank, John T.	9th	Infantry	NJ	Co H
Freeman, Charles	31st	Infantry	NJ	Co H
Freeman, Enos E.	15th	Infantry	NJ	Co G
Freeman, Thomas	9th	Infantry	NJ	Co K
Frost, Henry	10th	Infantry	NJ	Co H
Fulton, John	22nd	Infantry	NJ	Co A
Giles, James	14th	Infantry	NJ	Co C
Goodwin, George	3rd	Infantry	NJ	Co I
	35th	Infantry	NJ	Co D
Gould, George	9th	Infantry	NJ	Co C
	10th	Infantry	NJ	Co A
Gould, William J.	26th	Infantry	NJ	Co F

Graham, Robert	9th	Infantry	NJ	Co A
Gregory, John	28th	Infantry	NJ	Co F
Gregory, Thomas R.	15th	Infantry	NJ	Co A
Hall, Francis	1st	Infantry	NJ	Co A
Hall, George	25th	Infantry	NJ	Co D
	9th	Infantry	NJ	Co D
Hall, James	13th	Infantry	NJ	Co E
	2nd	Infantry	NJ	Co E
	28th	Infantry	NJ	Co E
Hand, Edward Scott	14th	Infantry	NJ	Co E
Hand, James	14th	Infantry	NJ	Co G
Hand, Jesse	14th	Infantry	NJ	Co E
Hand, John	3rd	Infantry	NJ	Co I
Hand, William	11th	Infantry	NJ	Co BI
Harvey, John H.	14th	Infantry	NJ	Co E
Hedden, Jacob	8th	Infantry	NJ	Co I
Hedden, William	3rd	Infantry	NJ	Co I
Henry, Henry	162nd	Infantry	NJ	Co A
Henry, John Lewis	14th	Infantry	NJ	Co C
Henry, Thomas	3rd	Infantry	NJ	Co D
Henry, William	14th	Infantry	NJ	Co C
Higgins, David S. C.	9th	Infantry	NJ	Co K
Higgins, Thomas	22nd	Infantry	NJ	Co H
Hoff, John	31st	Infantry	NJ	Co A
Holland, Abraham	30th	Infantry	NJ	Co C
Holland, George	1st	Cavalry	NJ	Co C
Holston, John M.	9th	Infantry	NJ	Co KG
Hubbard, James Frank	30th	Infantry	NJ	Co H
Hughes, Hugh	2nd	Infantry	NJ	Co A
	40th	Infantry	NJ	Co D
Hunt, Jacob	4th	Infantry	NJ	?
Hunt, Jacob	30th	Infantry	NJ	Co E
	1st	Battalion	NJ	Co A
Hunt, James	1st	Cavalry	NJ	Co I
Hunt, Thomas	5th	Infantry	NJ	Co A
Jackson, Andrew	34th	Infantry	NJ	Co F
Jackson, John K.	9th	Infantry	NJ	Co K

Jackson, Thomas R.	3rd	Infantry	NJ	Co H
	4th	Infantry	NJ	Co F
Jewell, Edward	8th	Infantry	NJ	Co I
Johnson, John H.	5th	Infantry	NJ	Co H
Johnson, John L.	1st	Infantry	NJ	Co I
Johnson, William H.	9th	Infantry	NJ	Co G
Johnson, William M.	9th	Infantry	NJ	Co KC
Jones, Edward	14th	Infantry	NJ	Co C
Jones, Obadiah	14th	Infantry	NJ	Co E
Jones, Williams	14th	Infantry	NJ	Co C
Kane, John	9th	Infantry	NJ	Co K
Kellum, Josiah	9th	Infantry	NJ	Co K
Kent, Henry C.	11th	Infantry	NJ	Co D
Kennedy, Daniel	9th	Infantry	NJ	Co G
King, Joseph H.	9th	Infantry	NJ	Co H
	35th	Infantry	NJ	Co A
Kinsey, George	30th	Infantry	NJ	Co C
	13th	Infantry	NJ	Co D
Kinsey, Peter	26th	Infantry	NJ	Co A
	13th	Infantry	NJ	Co A
Kinsey, William Baker	40th	Infantry	NJ	Co G
Layton, Samuel	2nd	Cavalry	NJ	Co M
Lee, Peter	2nd	Cavalry	NJ	Co D
Littell, William	3rd	Infantry	NJ	Co G
Little, Henry	29th	Infantry	NJ	Co F
Little, Isaac	9th	Infantry	NJ	Co F
Little, Jacob	14th	Infantry	NJ	Co E
Little, James	14th	Infantry	NJ	Co E
Long, John W.	14th	Infantry	NJ	Co E
Long, William	9th	Infantry	NJ	Co C
	7th	Infantry	NJ	Co G
Love, Marshall	39th	Infantry	NJ	Co K
Manning, William Henry	123rd	Infantry	NJ	Co A
Marsh, Charles	39th	Infantry	NJ	Co G
Marsh, Joseph N.	14th	Infantry	NJ	Co E
Marsh, Joseph R.	1st	Cavalry	NJ	Co K
Marsh, Randolph	2nd	Infantry	NJ	Co C

Marsh, Silas	30th	Infantry	NJ	Co C
Marsh, Solomon H.	8th	Infantry	NJ	Co I
Marsh, Stephen	40th	Infantry	NJ	Co C
Marsh, William G.	30th	Infantry	NJ	Co C
Marsh, William R.	14th	Infantry	NJ	Co E
Martin, John V.	14th	Infantry	NJ	Co C
Maxwell, Henry T.	9th	Infantry	NJ	Co K
McDonald, John	9th	Infantry	NJ	Co G
McFarland, Henry	8th	Infantry	NJ	Co I
Miller, John I.	5th	Infantry	NJ	Co H
Miller, John V.	1st	Infantry	NJ	Co A
Morse, Joseph E.	39th	Infantry	NJ	Co K
Morse, William	3rd	Cavalry	NJ	Co F
Mulford, Isaac	3rd	Cavalry	NJ	Co A
Mulford, John K.	10th	Infantry	NJ	Co B
	7th	Infantry	NJ	Co C
Mulligan, Charles	26th	Infantry	NJ	Co E
Murray, John F.	9th	Infantry	NJ	Co K
Murray, Samuel	9th	Infantry	NJ	Co G
Murray, Thomas	11th	Infantry	NJ	Co E
Nelson, James H. C.	26th	Infantry	NJ	Co C
	9th	Infantry	NJ	Co K
Newbern, William H.	9th	Infantry	NJ	Co KA
Noe, Dallas	2nd	Cavalry	NJ	Co A
	5th	Infantry	NJ	Co H
Noe, Elmer	14th	Infantry	NJ	Co E
Noe, Smith H.	5th	Infantry	NJ	Co H
Nun, Henry	9th	Infantry	NJ	Co G
Oliver, Jeremiah	1st	Infantry	NJ	Co B
Parker, Edward	23rd	Infantry	NJ	Co G
Parker, John	9th	Infantry	NJ	Co KA
Patterson, William	28th	Infantry	NJ	Co F
Peach, Frederick G.	9th	Infantry	NJ	Co G
Peacock, John	9th	Infantry	NJ	Co K
Pennington, Nathan	28th	Infantry	NJ	Co C
Perkins, John	34th	Infantry	NJ	Co D
Phillips, James P.	8th	Infantry	NJ	Co I

Post, Jacob	22nd	Infantry	NJ	Co A
Potter, David	14th	Infantry	NJ	Co E
Potter, George N.	2nd	Infantry	NJ	Co A
Potter, Henry L.	7th	Infantry	NJ	Co K
Potter, John W.	14th	Infantry	NJ	Co KF
Potter, William E	12th	Infantry	NJ	Co KG
Powell, William H.	1st	Cavalry	NJ	Co A
Powers, John S.	11th	Infantry	NJ	Co B
Price, John E.	9th	Infantry	NJ	Co K
Price, John H.	3rd	Infantry	NJ	Co K
Peer/Pur, Tunis	9th	Infantry	NJ	Co K
Quinn, James	8th	Infantry	NJ	Co H
	9th	Infantry	NJ	Co C
	9th	Infantry	NJ	Co K
Rae, Augustus	11th	Infantry	NJ	Co H
Randolph, Charles H.	30th	Infantry	NJ	Co H
	4th	Infantry	NJ	Co A
Randolph, Joseph C.	30th	Infantry	NJ	Co H
Randolph, William B.	1st	Light Artillery	NJ	Co B
Randolph, William H.	6th	Infantry	NJ	Co K
	8th	Infantry	NJ	Co G
Reed, David	9th	Infantry	NJ	Co KG
Rickets, John W.	9th	Infantry	NJ	Co K
Riley, James	9th	Infantry	NJ	Co G
Riley, Michael	1st	Artillery	NJ	Bat'y B
Roberts, Samuel L.	15th	Infantry	NJ	Co K
	10th	Infantry	NJ	Co C
	2nd	Infantry	NJ	Co I
Robinson, John Howard	7th	Infantry	NJ	Co G
Robinson, Samuel I.	11th	Infantry	NJ	Co E
Robinson, Thomas Peter	6th	Infantry	NJ	Co H
	40th	Infantry	NJ	Co A
Rose, Henry T.	14th	Infantry	NJ	Co E
Rose, Royal H.	30th	Infantry	NJ	Co H
Ross, James	15th	Infantry	NJ	Co B
	2nd	Infantry	NJ	Co I
Ryan, John R. T.	4th	Infantry	NJ	Co A

Name	Regiment	Branch	State	Company
Ryno, John	14th	Infantry	NJ	Co E
Ryno, William	2nd	Infantry	NJ	Co D
Sax, Henry	5th	Infantry	NJ	Co H
Schenk, Henry F.	9th	Infantry	NJ	Co E
Schenk, Peter	15th	Infantry	NJ	Co E
Scott, Charles H.	24th	Infantry	NJ	Co I
	33	Infantry	NJ	Co C
Scott, William A.	1st	Infantry	NJ	Co A
Simmonds, John W.	9th	Infantry	NJ	Co K
Simmons, Thomas S.	84th	Infantry	NJ	Co B
Slater, Edward	14th	Infantry	NJ	Co C
Slater, Samuel	30th	Infantry	NJ	Co H
Smith, George	9th	Infantry	NJ	Co G
Smith, James	9th	Infantry	NJ	Co K
Smith, John W. B.	11th	Infantry	NJ	Co B
Smith, William M.	9th	Infantry	NJ	Co G
Stansbury, Joseph S.	1st	Infantry	NJ	Co G
Stewart, William Scott	40th	Infantry	NJ	Co D
Sutton, Aaron	11th	Infantry	NJ	Co B
Sutton, Charles	14th	Infantry	NJ	Co D
Taylor, Charles H.	8th	Infantry	NJ	Co I
Terhune, Cornelius	23rd	Infantry	NJ	Co H
Terhune, David B.	22nd	Infantry	NJ	Co C
Terhune, John W.	11th	Infantry	NJ	Co D
	21st	Infantry	NJ	Co H
Terhune, Martin	22nd	Infantry	NJ	Co A
Thompson, Rev. Thomas	9th	Infantry	NJ	Co G
Thorn, Randolph	30th	Infantry	NJ	Co H
	1st	Light Artillery	NJ	Co D
Thornton, George	2nd	Cavalry	NJ	Co F
Till, Samuel M.	13th	Infantry	NJ	Co K
Tilton, Henry	11th	Infantry	NJ	Co B
Tooker, Nathan	2nd	Infantry	NJ	Co A
Turner, Samuel	13th	Infantry	NJ	Co B
	33rd	Infantry	NJ	
	Unassigned			
	8th	Infantry	NJ	Co I

Tuttle, George	27th	Infantry	NJ	Co E
Vanderhoven, Jessie	30th	Infantry	NJ	Co C
	1st Light Artillery		NJ	Bat'y D
Vanderveer, Peter	70th	Infantry	NJ	Co K
	38th	Infantry	NJ	Co A
Vanderveer, William H.	29th	Infantry	NJ	Co F
	32nd	Infantry	NJ	Co G
Van Horn, John W.	14th	Infantry	NJ	Co A
	6th	Infantry	NJ	Co B
Van Horn, William H.	2nd	Infantry	NJ	Co A
Van Houten, James C.	14th	Infantry	NJ	Co C
Van Houton, John J.	22nd	Infantry	NJ	Co A
Vannaman, William	30th	Infantry	NJ	Co C
Van Pelt, David H.	11th	Infantry	NJ	Co B
Van Pelt, Jacob D.	11th	Infantry	NJ	Co B
Van Pelt, Jeremiah	11th	Infantry	NJ	Co B
Van Riper, John	27th	Infantry	NJ	Co G
Van Sickles, Albert	14th	Infantry	NJ	Co E
Vermeule, Nathan P.	30th	Infantry	NJ	Co H
Voorhees, Charles A.	11th	Infantry	NJ	Co B
Voorhees, Edmund A.	14th	Infantry	NJ	Co C
Voorhees, Henry	9th	Infantry	NJ	Co C
Voorhees, Jeremiah	11th	Infantry	NJ	Co A
Voorhees, John C.	11th	Infantry	NJ	Co B
Voorhis, Nicholas	22nd	Infantry	NJ	Co A
Walker, Thomas	14th	Infantry	NJ	Co C
Wallace, John	13th	Infantry	NJ	Co K
Ward, Charles	9th	Infantry	NJ	Co G
	Wagoner			
Ward, John	9th	Infantry	NJ	Co K
	14th	Infantry	NJ	Co I
Ward, Thomas	14th	Infantry	NJ	Co E
Ward, William	9th	Infantry	NJ	Co G
	1st	Light Artillery	NJ	Co E
Watson, George	3rd	Infantry	NJ	Co K
Watson, Thomas	14th	Infantry	NJ	Co I
White, Charles	9th	Infantry	NJ	Co K

White, George	14th	Infantry	NJ	Co G
White, James	35th	Infantry	NJ	Co H
Whitehead, George	9th	Infantry	NJ	Co K
Whitehead, James	13th	Infantry	NJ	Co K
Whitney, George	9th	Infantry	NJ	Co G
Williams, Charles	9th	Infantry	NJ	Co K
Williams, Frederick	38th	Infantry	NJ	Co K
Williams, James H.	9th	Infantry	NJ	Co G
Williams, Robert S.	9th	Infantry	NJ	Co K
Williams, William H.	9th	Infantry	NJ	Co A
Wills, William H.	24th	Infantry	NJ	Co B
Wilson, Henry	2nd	Infantry	NJ	Co A
Wilson, Henry F.	14th	Infantry	NJ	Co C
Wilson, James	5th	Infantry	NJ	Co H
Winans, Alfred L.	11th	Infantry	NJ	Co D
Winans, Theodore	13th	Infantry	NJ	Co B
Wood, Amos	29th	Infantry	NJ	Co F
Wood, Henry	10th	Infantry	NJ	Co I
Woods, Charles	3rd	Infantry	NJ	Co K
Wright, Edward	21st	Infantry	NJ	Co H
Wright, James	3rd	Infantry	NJ	Co C
Wyckoff, Benjamin	31st	Infantry	NJ	Co A

.

NEW YORK

Abers, Charles	5th	Cavalry	NY	Co L
	Blacksmith			
Abbott, Charles	2nd	Mounted Rifles	NY	?
	Teamster			
Abrams, William	1st	Mounted Rifles	NY	Co M
	Teamster			
Abrams, Henry	63rd	Infantry	NY	Co E
Adair, James	16th	Cavalry	NY	Co B
	Teamster			
Adams, Lorain	16th	Cavalry	NY	G
	Farrier			

Name	Regiment		State	Company
Adams, Thomas	57th	Infantry	NY	Co D
	Teamster			
Adams, William	160th	Infantry	NY	Co K
Adkins, Peter	133rd	Infantry	NY	Co. F
	Teamster			
Aetheridge, March	89th	Infantry	NY	?
Alexander, James	128th	Infantry	NY	Co G
	Teamster			
Alexander, Joseph	50th	Infantry	NY	Co A
	Teamster			
Allen, Asbury	142nd	Infantry	NY	Co D
Alstine, Thomas Van	25th	Infantry	NY	Co I
	Teamster			
Ambs, Fred John	52nd	Infantry	NY	Co H
	Teamster			
Ani, Daniel	14th	Cavalry	NY	Co BA
	Saddler			
Antrim, Watson	6th Light Artillery		NY Ind. Bat'y	
Appo, William	30th	Infantry	NY	Co I
Asberry Allen	142nd	Infantry	NY	Co D
Ark, George	18th	Cavalry	NY	CoB
	Teamster			
Atkinson, Thomas	1st M'td. Rifles		NY	Co GE
	Saddler			
Austin, William	50th	Infantry	NY	Co F
	Teamster			
Babbitt, Putnam P.	11th	Cavalry	NY	Co G
	Saddler			
Babcock, Alphonzo	3rd	Cavalry	NY	Co D,L
	Saddler			
Ballou, Asa	2nd	Cavalry	NY	Co H
	Teamster/Saddler			
Ballou, Henry	22nd	Cavalry	NY	Co M
	Saddler			
Barker, Samuel	3rd	Cavalry	NY	Co H
	Saddler			
Bennett, George W.	6th Light Artillery		NY Ind. Bat'y	

Bergman, Godfrey/Gotfred	7th	Infantry	NY	Co A
	Teamster			
Bischer, Eliphalet	5th	Infantry	NY	Co C
	Teamster			
Bishop, William	6th	Light Artillery	NY	Ind. Bat'y
Branch/Brunt, George W.	6th	Light Artillery	NY	Ind. Bat'y
Branch/Brunt, Harvey	6th	Light Artillery	NY	Ind. Bat'y
Brandt, Henry	54th	Infantry	NY	?
Brown, George Henry	6th	Light Artillery	NY	Ind. Bat'y
Brown, George Washington	6th	Light Artillery	NY	Ind. Bat'y
Bulstein, Nicholas	23rd	Cavalry	NY	Co A
	Saddler			
Carle, Thomas	52nd	Infantry	NY	Co B
Calkins, James	13th	Cavalry	NY	Co E,K
	Farrier			
Calkins, James	3rd	Cavalry Prov.	NY	Co K
Cameron, James	3rd	Cavalry	NY	Co E
	Farrier			
Clark, Moses P.	6th	Light Artillery	NY	Ind. Bat'y
Conover, William W.	14th	Infantry	NY	Co I
Cooper, Abraham	53rd	Infantry (1st)	NY	Co H
	Teamster			
Dabony, Anthony	12th	Infantry	IN	Co D
	Teamster			
Freeman, Eul	6th	Light Artillery	NY	Ind. Bat'y
High, David I.	6th	Light Artillery	NY	Ind. Bat'y
Hughes, William H.	6th	Light Artillery	NY	Ind. Bat'y
Jackson, Abner	169th	Infantry	NY	?
	Transferred to U.S.C.T.			
Leonard, Charles	6th	Light Artillery	NY	Ind. Bat'y
Marsh, Edwin	6th	Light Artillery	NY	Ind. Bat'y
Marsh, Ellis	6th	Light Artillery	NY	Ind. Bat'y
Martin, John W.	6th	Light Artillery	NY	Ind. Bat'y
Martin, Joseph W.	6th	Light Artillery	NY	Ind. Bat'y
McCrossen, Thomas H.	6th	Light Artillery	NY	Ind. Bat'y
McDonald, John	6th	Light Artillery	NY	Ind. Bat'y
Miller, Cornelius	6th	Light Artillery	NY	Ind. Bat'y

Plum, George M., Jr.	6th Light Artillery		NY Ind. Bat'y	
Potter, John W.	6th Light Artillery		NY Ind. Bat'y	
Potter, Joseph M.	6th Light Artillery		NY Ind. Bat'y	
Randolph, Theodore	6th Light Artillery		NY Ind. Bat'y	
Simms, John W.	6th Light Artillery		NY Ind. Bat'y	
Thorn, Thompson	6th Light Artillery		NY Ind. Bat'y	
Aetheridge, March	89th	Infantry	NY	?
Babbitt, Putnam P.	11th	Cavalry	NY	Co G
	Saddler			
Backus, Robert	13th	Cavalry	NY	Co F
	Teamster			
Baker, Levi	59th	Infantry	NY	Co I
	Teamster			
Baker, Robinson	136th	Infantry	NY	Co H
	Teamster			
Ballou, Asa	2nd	Cavalry	NY	Co H
	Teamster/Saddler			
Ballou, Henry	22nd	Cavalry	NY	Co M
	Saddler			
Barker, Samuel	3rd	Cavalry	NY	Co H
	Saddler			
Berthold, Adler	3rd Provincial Cav.		NY	Co L
	Farrier			
Brady, James	118th	Infantry	NY	Co C
Brady, Samuel	118th	Infantry	NY	Co C
		Transferred to	20th	USCT
Brody, Alexander	165	Infantry	NY	Co C
Brown, Peter	164th	Infantry	NY	Co H
Brum, Ira	185th	Infantry	NY	Co F
Bulstein, Nicholas	23rd	Cavalry	NY	Co A
	Saddler			
Calkins, James	13th	Cavalry	NY	Co E,K
	Farrier			
Cameron, James	3rd	Cavalry	NY	Co E
	Farrier			
Carolina, Lecrett	1st	Engineers	NY	Co H
Chester, Washington	26	Ind. Battery	NY	?

Crowley, Thomas A.	4th	Infantry	NY	Co E
Day, Edward I.	70th	Infantry	NY	Co K
	86th	Infantry	NY	Co C
DeHart, John W.	9th	Infantry	NY	Co B
DeHart, William Cherwood	7th	Infantry	NY	Co F
Dhu, Dennis	91st	Infantry	NY	Co B
Dickerson, William A.	10th	Light Art'y	NY	?
Doty, John H.	70th	Infantry	NY	Co K
Dow, Edward S.	5th	Infantry	NY	Co I
	14th	Cavalry	NY	Co K
Dunham, David B.	44th	Infantry	NY	Co I
Esterbrooks, Edward M.	44th	Infantry	NY	Co B
Fox, John P.	10th	Heavy Art'y	NY	Co H
Godfrey, William	169th	Infantry	NY	Co E
Green, Samuel K.	1st	Engineers	NY	Co A
Hand, Henry Wells	136th	Infantry	NY	Co F
Henry, Henry	162nd	Infantry	NY	Co A
Jackson, Alexander	169th	Infantry	NY	
		Transferred to 31st USCT		
Jackson, Abner	169th	Infantry	NY	
		Transferred to 31st USCT		
Jackson, Damion	169th	Infantry	NY	
		Transferred to 31st USCT		
Jackson, Virgil	169th	Infantry	NY	
Lamb, William	123rd	Infantry	NY	
		Transferred to 39th USCT		
Marsh, Robert	86th	Infantry	NY	Co F
	136th	Infantry	NY	Co G
Morris, Cornelius	177th	Infantry	NY	Co B
	178th	Infantry	NY	Co A
Murry, William	18th	Infantry	NY	Co D
Olmstead, William H..	2nd	Heavy Art'y	NY	Co H
Parker, James E.	9th	Heavy Art'y	NY	Co B
Pernell, Jacob	91st	Infantry	NY	Co B
Perry, Jerry	187th	Infantry	NY	Co K
Potter, Edward C.	173 rd	Infantry	NY	Co C
Potter, George	117th	Infantry	NY	Co G

Provost, William W.	134th	Infantry	NY	
	Unassigned			
Randolph, James F.	70th	Infantry	NY	Co D
Randolph, William B.	12th	Light Art'y	NY	?
	5th	Light Art'y	U.S. Army	Bat'y C
Ray, John H.	43rd	Infantry	NY	Co I
Reynolds, Ashley	99th	Infantry	NY	Co B
Reynolds, Ashley	132nd	Infantry	NY	Co H
Robinson, Rufus	121st	Infantry	NY	Co D
Roll, John K.	52nd	Infantry	NY	Co C
Ropes, Elihu .	11th	Ind. Att'y	NY	?
Schenck, John Henry	70th	Infantry	NY	Co D
Simmons, Ned	155th	Infantry	NY	Co D
Stanford, Henry	101st	Infantry	NY	Co A
Stewart, John E.	44th	Infantry	NY	Co D
Still, Charles R.	82nd	Infantry	NY	Co K
Sutton, Benjamin	67th	Infantry	NY	Co H
Thomas, Calvin	161	Infantry	NY	Co A
Van Campen, Eugene	1st	Heavy Art'y	NY	Co A
Vanderveer, Peter	70th	Infantry	NY	Co E
Vanderveer, William H.	32nd	Infantry	NY	Co G
Van Pelt, George	4th	Heavy Art'y	NY	Co E
Victor, Ela	133rd	Infantry	NY	Co F
Voorhees, Jeremiah	11th	Infantry	NY	Co B
Voorhees, Jeremiah F.	9th	Infantry	NY	Co A
Washington, Williams	51st	Infantry	NY	Co E
White, Charles	9th	Militia	NY	Co K
White, Louis	14th	Heavy Art'y	NY	Co H
Williams, Edward	132	Infantry	NY	Co H
Wilson, Andrew	159th	Infantry	NY	Co H
Wyckoff, Charles	48th	Infantry	NY	Co HA
Zabriske, Jacob H.	114th	Infantry	NY	Co D

NORTH CAROLINA

Carter, John W.	3rd	Infantry	NC	Co D
	Teamster		Mounted	

OHIO

Name	Unit		State	Company
Amend, Michael	3rd	Cavalry	OH	Co L
	Saddler			
Angle/Angel, James M.	7th	Infantry	OH	Co I
	Teamster/Farrier			
Artist, Andrew	7th	Cavalry	OH	Co G
	Saddler			
Baker, Jeremiah	9th	Cavalry	OH	Co H
	Farrier			
Barker, John	1st	Cavalry	OH	Co B
	Farrier			
Barker, John H.	12th	Cavalry	OH	Co C
	Saddler			
Baumann, Louis	4th	Cavalry	OH	Co E
	Teamster			
Baumgardner, Isaiah	8th	Cavalry	OH	Co A
	Farrier			
Baumgardner, Henry	10th	Cavalry	OH	Co A
	Farrier			
Bawker/Boker, Oscar P.	9th	Cavalry	OH	Co G
	Teamster			
Bayer/Boyer, Henry M.	9th	Cavalry	OH	Co G
	Teamster			
Beatty/Beaty, William V.	81st	Infantry	OH	Co G
	Teamster			
Beatty, Wilson	4th	Cavalry	OH	Co D,I
	Teamster			
Beggs, James	5thI. Batt'yCavalry		OH	Co A
	Blacksmith/Farrier			
Brown, Milton A.	100th	Infantry	OH	Co E
Bruster, John	33rd	Infantry	OH	Co A
	Teamster			
Burghhardt, Henry	5th	Cavalry	OH	Co D
	Saddler			
Butler, Barkley	141st	Infantry	OH	Co F
	Teamster			

Name	Unit		State	Company
Caine, Edmond	5th	Cavalry	OH	Co F
	Saddler			
Cameron, Archibald	5th	Cavalry	OH	Co K
	Farrier			
Clingle, Samuel	56th	Infantry	OH	Co E,B
	Teamster			
Colby, James	54th	Infantry	OH	Co B
Croshon, Rev. David R.	141st	Infantry	OH	Co H
Davis, John W.	121st	Infantry	OH	Co B
Ellert, Wilburn	74th	Infantry	OH	Co K
Evans, Wilson B.	178th	Infantry	OH	Co D
Evans, Wilson B.	186th	Infantry	OH	?
Kittera, James	89th	Infantry	OH	Co K
Pender, Pattie	46th	Infantry	OH	?
Sales, James	88th	Infantry	OH	Co C
	69th	Infantry	OH	Co C
Smith, Sandy	10	Infantry	OH	Co K
Strander, Erren	69th	Infantry	OH	?

PENNSYLVANIA

Name	Unit		State	Company
Ackerman, George W.	1st	Light Artillery	PA	Bat'y F
Ambuster, Jacob	5th	Cavalry	PA	Co G
	Saddler			
Ash, George W.	119th	Infantry	PA	Co D
Atwood/Attwood, Daniel	23rd	Infantry	PA	Co R
	Teamster			
Balliet, Edward	19th	Cavalry	PA	Co K
	Farrier			
Baxter, Gilbert	7th	Cavalry	PA	Co C
	Saddler			
Beam, Daniel	101st	Infantry	PA	Co D
	Teamster			
Beam, Daniel	55th	Infantry	PA	?
	Teamster			
Beam, Robert C.	14th	Cavalry	PA	Co D
	Teamster			

Bear, Samuel	79th Cavalry Teamster	PA	Co C
Beck, Henry R.	23rd Infantry Teamster	PA	Co A
Bedgar, John	17th Infantry Teamster	PA	Co E
Burns, James	16th Cavalry Teamster	PA	Co B
Bishop, James C.	21st Cavalry Saddler	PA	Co G
Bowman, John	4th Cavalry Teamster	OH	Co E
Boyer, George	110th Infantry Teamster	PA	Co G
Boyer, George	105th Infantry Teamster	PA	Co I
Boyer, Henry	9th Cavalry Teamster	PA	Co G
Bedlow, John	124th Cavalry Teamster	PA	Co F
Bertram, Peter	208th Infantry Teamster	PA	Co B
Bishop, James C.	21st Cavalry Saddler	PA	Co G
Borland, James W.	23rd Infantry Teamster	PA	Co K
Bruster, John	33rd Infantry Teamster	OH	Co A
Butler, Benjamin I.	19th Cavalry Saddler	PA	Co C
Bullman, John	14th Cavalry Saddler	PA	Co L
Bullmer, William	1st Prov'l Cavalry Saddler	PA	Co K
Caldwell, James	15th Cavalry Farrier	PA	Co B
Capp, John M.	132nd Infantry Teamster	PA	Co K

Cole, Jabez C.	52nd Infantry	PA	Co I
Costello, Edward	66th Infantry	PA	Co K
	Teamster		
Cowdon, James Seneca	85th Infantry	PA	Co A
	Teamster		
Dener, Christian	48th Infantry	PA	Co D
	Teamster		
Foreman, Isaac	35th Infantry	PA	Co C
Godshalk, Samuel	104th Infantry	PA	Co B
Jackson, William H.	43rd Light Art'y	PA	Co D
Leeds, Henry H.	6th Cavalry	PA	?
McDonald, John	12th Cavalry	PA	Co F
Ramsey, William	96th Infantry	PA	?
Reese, Samuel W.	1st Cavalry	PA	Co G
Robeson, Philip	55th Infantry	PA	Co H
Robeson, Toby	55th Infantry	PA	Co H
Stagner, Barclay	8th Cavalry	PA	Co M
Steward, Stephen	7th Cavalry	PA	Co K
Stewart, William Scott	83rd Infantry	PA	?
	123rd Infantry	PA	?
	Ass/t Surgeon		

RHODE ISLAND

Debois, Edward M.	14th Heavy Art'y	RI	Co B
Reeder, James	1st Light Art'y	RI	Co I

TENNESSEE

Amburn, Samuel	10th Cavalry	TN	Co I
	Saddler		
Ballard, Sampson	10th Cavalry	TN	Co B
	Farrier		
Bishop, Abner	12th Cavalry	TN	Co F
	Saddler		
Bradley, William	6th Cavalry	TN	Co B
	Teamster		

Calhoun, Thomas C.	7th Farrier	Cavalry	TN	Co I
Haverston, Thomas	10th	Cavalry	TN	Co B

VERMONT

Adkins, Jacob	52nd Teamster	Infantry	IL	Co F

WEST VIRGINIA

Ankeney, Henry	3rd Saddler	Cavalry	WV	Co F
Buckbee, James A.	2nd Saddler	Cavalry	WV	Co I

WISCONSIN

Collins, Isaac	38th	Infantry	WI	Co H
Daniels, Alva	1st Teamster	Cavalry	WI	Co H
McDade, James	4th	Cavalry	WI	Co F
Weeks, Thomas	31st	Infantry	WI	Co A

UNITED STATES ARMY

Adams, John	3rd U.S. Cavalry Blacksmith		Co I G
Crite, Rohan	U.S	Army	
Carroll, Robert	U.S. Hospital Steward	Army	
Dunham, Enoch	15th U.S Infantry	Army	Co G

FINAL RESTING PLACES

Pvt. Philip Ackerman 5th N.J. Infantry	Evergreen Cemetery Hillside, New Jersey
Pvt. Asberry Allen 142nd N.Y. Vols.	Lake View Cemetery Saline County, Ilinois
Pvt. Bruce Anderson 142nd N.Y. Infantry	Greenhill Cemetery Amsterdam, New York.
Corporal William Appo 30th N.Y. Infantry	Bull Run Battlefield Manassas, Virginia
Pvt.Taylor Bowen	Wesleyan Cemetery Cincinnati, Ohio
Pvt. Ira Brum 185th N.Y. Infantry	Ithaca City Cemetery Ithaca, New York
Pvt. Henry (Hanry) Clay	Wesleyan Cemetery Cincinnati, Ohio
Pvt. Charles Graffell 2nd California Cavalry	Oak Hill Cemetery Red Bluffs, California
Pvt. William D. Fox 2nd Michigan Cavalry Co F	Highland Cemetery Ypsilanti, Michigan
Pvt. Richard B. Gordon	Wesleyan Cemetery Cininnati, Ohio
Pvt. Thomas Eston Hemings 175th Ohio Infantry	Andersonville Prison Andersonville, Georgia
Pvt. Aquilla Lett 13th Michigan Infantry	Arlington Cemetery Van Buren County, Michigan

Pvt. Amos McKinney 1st Alabama Cavalry	Magnolia-Sykes Cemetery Decatur, Alabama
Pvt. Debrix Miller 4th Michigan Infantry	Greenwood Cemetery Hillsdale, Michigan
Pvt. William Norman	Morgan Bethel Cemetery Lambert, Ohio
Pvt. Crowder Patience 103rd PA Infantry	West Pittston Cemetery West Pittston, Pennsylvania
Pvt. Thomas Patience 5th Mass. Cavalry	Chowan Country Gravesite unknown
Pvt. Samuel James Patterson 5th Mass. Cavalry	Wilkes-Barre City Cemetery Wilkes-Barre, Pennsylvania
Private John Rolack 85th NY Infantry	Andersonville Prison Andersonville, Georgia
Pvt. Barclay Stagner 8th PA Infantry	Hatboro Baptist Cemetery Hatboro, Penna.
Pvt. George Washington (1)	Wesleyan Cemetery Cincinnati, Ohio
Pvt. George Washington (2)	Wesleyan Cemetery Cincinnati, Ohio
Pvt. Simon West 1st Alabama Cavalry	Highland Park Cemetery Warrenville, Ohio
Private John Yates	Wesleyan Cemetery Cincinnati, Ohio

END NOTES

1. *War of the Rebellion: Official Records of the Union and Confederate Armies.*
2. "Patriots" served as volunteers and were not members of the regular Army.
3. The Emancipation Proclamation was signed by President Abraham Lincoln on 1 January 1863.
4. *War of the Rebellion: Official Records of the Union and Confederate Armies.*
5. United States Colored Troops (U.S.C.T.) were to be led by white officers only.
6. Belinda Hurmence, *My Folks Don't Want Me to Talk About Slavery*, John F. Blair, Publisher, Winston-Salem, N.C., 1999.
7. Donald M. Wisnoski, *The Opportunity is at Hand: Oneida County, New York Colored Soldiers in the Civil War*, Schroeder Publications, Lynchburg, Virginia, 2003, p. 97.
8. Ethel M. Washington, *Union County's Black Soldiers and Sailors of the Civil War,* The History Press, Charleston, S.C., 2011, p. 144.
9. *Ancestry.com* Soldier Search.
10. Washington, p. 196.
11. William Henry Johnson, *Autobiography of Dr. William H. Johnson*, N.Y.: Haskell House Publishers, 1900, p. 17.
12. The *Pine and Palm* was a Boston publication advocating emigration and colonization of Blacks to such places as Haiti.
13. William Henry Johnson was a barber with a lucrative business in Albany, N.Y. His autobiography details his various efforts for improving the lives of Blacks in his city.
14. *Ancestry.com* Soldier Search.
15. "Contraband" referred to run-away slaves, also called refugees, who escaped to the invading Yankees.
16. General Orders No.143.
17. Letter to the editor of the *Civil War News*, William Gladstone, January 2005.
18. 1st Kansas Colored Infantry skirmished with a unit of Rebel guerillas on 29 October 1862 at Island Mound, Missouri,

thereby giving it the distinction of being the first Black unit to skirmish with the enemy.

19. 1st South Carolina had been formed before 1st Kansas, but had not been reorganized soon enough to be recognized first.
20. Words from Douglass' address at a Meeting for the Promotion of Colored Enlistments, 6 July 1863, published in *Douglass' Monthly*, August 1863.
21. Courtesy of Robert Farrell.
22. Peggy Sawyer-Williams received the Genealogist of the Year Award for 2006 from the Library of Michigan, Lansing, Michigan. She is the immediate past president of the Fred Hart Williams Genealogical Society of Detroit, Michigan, and a member of Tent #3 of the Daughters of Union Veterans.
23. Pvt. Hopkins West information provided by Peggy Sawyer-Williams.
24. Pvt. Benjamin Guy information provided by Peggy Sawyer-Williams.
25. *Ancestry.com* Soldier Search.
26. Pvt. William Dudley Fox information provided by descendants Vivian Fox Porche and Maia Porche.
27. Pvt. Martin Scott information provided by Sheila Bourelly.
28. *War…Griffith Men Enlisted in the Colored Troops as Union Soldiers During the Civil War,* a publication provided by Sheila Bourelly.
29. Both Evans brothers participated in rescuing a fugitive slave who had been residing in Oberlin. Slave-catchers were about to ship John Price back to Kentucky, but 37 townsmen broke the Fugitive Slave Law by helping Price reach safety in Canada.
30. httpp://www.oberlin.edu/externa.l/EOG/CivilWarTour/Stop2.html
31. http://www.newyorkhistoryblog.com/2012/01/african-american-men-in-white-ny-civil.html
32. "*Asberry Allen, Civil War Veteran,*" Saline County, Illinois, submitted by Darrel Dexter, SAGA XXX/3, p. 19.

33. Pvt. William Appo, courtesy of John Carter and Joseph Romeo.
34. Pvt. Ephraim Pierce courtesy of Joan Bryant.
35. Pvt. Thomas Eston Hemings courtesy of Hari Jones, curator of the AACW Museum, Washington, D.C.
36. Andersonville NHS Civil War Research File Information Sheet has under "Remarks" that Thomas Eston Hemings was *"reported to be the grandson of Thomas Jefferson."*
http://www.pbs.org/wgbh/pages/frontline/shows/Jefferson/cron/1873marc.html
37. *Ibid.*
38. The Fugitive Slave Law (Act) was passed by the United States Government as part of the Compromise of 1850 between Northern Free-Soilers and Southern slave-holders.
39. The Academy award Best Movie *12 Years a Slave* released in 2014 illustrates how easily free Blacks could be kidnapped and sold into slavery.
40. "*A Sprig of Jefferson Was Eston Hemings,*" Scioto Gazette, Ohio, 1902.
41. en.wikepedia./org/wiki/John_Wayles_Jefferson
42. *Ancestry.com* Soldier Search.
43. Wisconsin Historical Society.
44. The South's "peculiar institution" was slavery and all that it entailed.
45. The "one drop policy" ruled that any person with at least one Black ancestor, no matter how many generations distant, is to be racially identified as Black.
46. "*Putting Together Pieces of a Civil War Puzzle,*" *Washington Post,* Timothy Wilson, 31 July 2008.
47. Pvt. Amos McKinney's granddaughter, great-grandson and great-great granddaughters.
48. 1st Alabama Cavalry was made up of die-hard "Unionists" who did not support the Confederacy.
49. Reporter describes the presence and roles of dignitaries, re-enactors, McKinney descendants, and others.
50. Reporter can be reached at Gloversville@leaderherald.com.
51. Information obtained at the African American Civil War Museum (AACWM) in Washington, D.C. where the name of

Pvt. Bruce Anderson is commemorated with the other Black Medal of Honor recipients.

52. Ambrose "Cowboy" Anderson, Jr. is the son of Ambrose Anderson, Sr., son of Pvt. Bruce Anderson.
53. *Ancestry.com* Soldier Search.
54. Flyers- www.pslweb.org/liberationnews/newspaper/vol-7-no-3/first-black-soldiers-recruited-into-civil-war-html
55. Young Col. Robert Gould Shaw was the son of staunch abolitionists in Boston, Massachusetts.
56. Sgt. William Carney won his Medal of Honor at the Battle of Battery Wagner (Fort Wagner), Charleston, S.C.
57. Photograph is of the replica at the National Gallery of Art in Washington, D.C.
58. Dudley Taylor Cornish, *The Sable Arm: Negro Troops in the Union Army, 1861-1865*, (N.Y.:W. W. Norton & Co., Inc., 1966).
59. Sgt. Major Christian Fleetwood received a Medal of Honor six months after Battle of Chaffin's Farm. After two color-bearers were shot he had seized the colors and he bore them nobly through the rest of the fight.
60. Allowed Blacks to enlist as undercooks in the regular Army.
61. Undercooks were to be listed at foot of roster.
62. Roster courtesy of Geoffrey Satter.
63. Muster record courtesy of Geoffrey Satter.
64. Weymouth Jordan and Gerald Thomas, "*Massacre at Plymouth,*" The North Carolina Historical Review, Vol. LXXII, No. Vol. 2, April 1995, p. 155.
65. Wayne Mahood, *The Plymouth Pilgrims: A History of the Eighty-Fifth New York Infantry in the Civil War*, Longstreet House, Hightstown, N. J., 1989, p. 197.
66. The Model 1858 Dress Hat named after William J. Hardee and was the regulation dress hat for enlisted men.
67. Jordan and Thomas, p. 175.
68. Wayne Mahood, *Charlie Mosher's Civil War: From Fair Oaks to Andersonville with the Plymouth Pilgrims (85th N.Y. Infantry),* Longstreet House, Hightstown, N.J., 1994, p. 205.

69. Pvt. John Rolack is the only known runaway slave buried at Andersonville Prison.
70. Bob O'Connor, *The U.S. Colored Troops at Andersonville Prison*, 2009.
71. At Ft. Pillow, Tennessee, on 12 April 1864, while attempting to surrender, Black soldiers were massacred by Confederate soldiers under the command of Major-General Nathan Bedford Forrest.
72. Courtesy of Harry Thompson, past curator of the Port O' Plymouth Museum, Plymouth, N.C.
73. *Ibid.*
74. *Roster of the 103rd Pennsylvania Regiment.*
75. Luther S. Dickey, *History of 103rd Regiment: Pennsylvania Veteran Volunteer Infantry 1861-1865,* L.S. Dickey, 1910, p. 51.
76. Courtesy of Sandra Panzitta, Research Assistant, Luzerne County Historical Society, Wilkes-Barre, Pennsylvania.
77. Correction—The Patience family lived on Tunkhannock Ave.
78. Correction—Three girls married and left the family homestead.
79. Correction—North Carolina, not South.
80. Correction—North Carolina, not South.
81. The symbol of the Grand Army of the Republic (G.A.R.) is a five-pointed star symbolizing the five branches of the Army (heavy and light artillery, cavalry, infantry, engineers).
82. Her mother's widow's pension record was with Aunt Lillie's momentos which she kept hidden in a small black tin box.
83. Filed at the War College at Carlisle Barracks.
84. *Ibid.*
85. *Ibid.*
86. *Ibid.*
87. *Ibid.*
88. Bennie McRae is a noted author, historian and veteran.
89. *The Roster of Union Soldiers 1861-1865,* a printed copy of the Index to the Compiled Military Service Records (CMSR), (Wilmington, N.C.: Broadfoot Publishing, 1998).

90. Glenda McWhither Todd is the regimental historian of the 1st Alabama Cavalry and author of *First Alabama Cavalry, USA: Homage to Patriotism.*
91. *Ancestry.com* U.S. Civil War Soldiers, 1861-1865.
92. *Ancestry.com*- using keyword "undercooks."
93. One of the sixteen 1st Alabama Cavalry Black cooks.
94. Participants: Re-enactors and Boy Scouts Troop 812—North Coast Ranger Academy.
95. Peggy Allen Towns is the author of *Duty Driven*; *The Plight of North Alabama's African Americans During the Civil War.*
96. Ethel Washington is the author of *Union County's Black Soldiers and Sailors of the Civil War.*
97. Reporter Dan Yount stated, "*Members of the First Masonic District of the Most Worshipful Prince Hall Grand Lodge of Ohio (an African American fraternal organization) and the First Masonic District of the Grand Lodge of Ohio Masons (the White Masonic organization) conducted a headstone dedication for local African American Civil War Veterans at the Wesleyan Cemetery at 4003 Colerain Ave. in the Northside neighborhood of Cincinnati on Sept. 28.*" 2013
98. The regiments are unknown to author.
99. http://theCincinnatiherald.com/news/2013/0ct/31/black-white-masons-mark-black-civil-war-vets-grave/?page#2
100. http://www.theintell.com/honoring-one-of-their-own/html_a7acbb2d-8407-570d-be39-2915ffbf9d2b.html
101. Washington, p. 65.
102. *Ibid.*
103. *Ancestry.com*
104. By request a Certificate of Honor will be created for each of the names inscribed on the Wall of Honor.
105. "Bound girls," oftentimes orphans, worked for an employer for a certain period of time.
106. John Hope Franklin & Loren Schweninger, "*Runaway Slaves: Rebels on the Plantation,*" Oxford University Press New York, N.Y., page 38.
107. Origin of "griot"— an African storyteller.

SOURCES

"African American Men in White N.Y. Civil War Units," Carol Kammer, New York History: *Historical News and Views From the Empire State.*

African American Perspectives: *Pamphlets from the Daniel A. P. Murray Collection,* 1818-1907.

"All Tom's Children: A President's presumed affair with a slave gives new meaning to the term Jeffersonian." Patrick Rogers, Glenn Garelik, Amanda Crawford, Bob Calandra, *People Magazine*, 11/23/98.

"A Sprig of Jefferson Was Eston Hemings." *Scipio Gazette*, 1902.

Bartlett, Captain A.W. *History of the 12th Regiment New Hampshire Volunteers in the War of the Rebellion.* Concord, N.H.: Ira C. Evans, 1897.

Bates, Samuel P. *History of Pennsylvania Volunteers, 1861-65.* Harrisburg, Pa.: B. Singerly, State Printer, Vol. 3, 1886-1871.

Civil War General News. September 1988.

"Civil War Veteran of Unusual Career is Valley Resident," *Sunday Independent,* Wilkes-Barre, Pennsylvania, 20 May 1928.

Cooper, Willie, *The Forgotten Legacy: The Black Soldiers and Sailors Who Fought in the Civil War, 1862-1866.* Jamaica, NY: Bravin Publishing, LLC, 2010.

Dickey, Luther S. *History of the 103rd Regiment: Pennsylvania Veteran Volunteer Infantry 1861-1865.* Chicago, Illinois: L.S. Dickey, 1910.

Franklin, John Hope and Moss, Alfred A. *From Slavery to Freedom: A History of African Americans*. 7th Edition, New York: McGraw-Hill, Inc., 1994.

Green, Robert Ewell. *Black Defenders of America 1775-1973*. Chicago: Johnson Publishing Co., Inc., 1974.

Hays, E.Z. *History of the 32nd Regiment: Ohio Veteran Volunteer Infantry*. Columbus, Ohio: Cott & Evans Printers, 1896.

Hays, Martin A. *A History of the 2nd Regiment New Hampshire Volunteers in the War of the Rebellion.* Lakeport, N.H., 1896.

"Jefferson's kin may have died at prison." Alia Beard, *Americus Times-Recorder,* 8/11/98.

Johnson, William Henry. *Autobiography of Dr. William Henry Johnson.* New York: Haskell House, Reprint of 1900 edition, 1970.

Jordan, Weymouth and Thomas, Gerald. "Massacre at Plymouth." *The North Carolina Historical Review*. Vol. LXXII, April 1995.

"Life among the Lowly," No. 1, Pike County (Ohio) Republican. 13 March 1873.

McPherson, James M. *Battle Cry for Freedom: The Civil War Era.* New York: Oxford University Press, 1998.

______. *The Negro's Civil War.* NY: Ballantine Books, 1965.

"More than 200 Gather to honor Civil War veteran," Deangelo McDaniel, *The Decatur Daily*, July 12, 2009.

O'Connor, Bob, *The U.S. Colored Troops at Andersonville Prison.* Infinity Publishing, West Conshohocken, Penna., 2009.

Patterson, Christine, *The Black Experience in Wyoming Valley.* Wilkes-Barre, Pa.: Wilkes College Press,.

Port-O' Plymouth Museum, Plymouth, N.C.

Redkey, Edwin S. *A Grand Army of Black Men.* Cambridge: Cambridge University Press, 1992.

Report of the Adjutant General of the State of Illinois, Vol. III. Revised by Brigadier General J. W. Vance, Adjutant General. Springfield, IL: H. W. Bokker, State Printer and Binder, 1886.

The Cincinnati Enquirer. "Cemeteries join fight to mark veterans' graves." Cindy Schroeder, 18 July 2013.

The Cincinnati Herald. "Black, White Masons mark Black Civil War vets'graves." Dan Yount, 31 October 2013.

The Roster of Union Soldiers 1861-65. Wilmington, N.C.: Broadfoot Publishers, 1998.

The Saga of Southern Illinois. "Asberry Allen Civil War Veteran," Darrel Dexter, SAGA XXX/3, p. 19.

Towns, Peggy Allen, *Duty Driven; The Plight of North Alabama's African Americans During the Civil War.* Bloomington: Author House, 2012.

"War…Griffin Men Enlisted in the Colored Troops as Union Soldiers During the Civil War."

War College at Carlisle Barracks, Harrisburg, Pennsylvania.

Washington, Ethel M., *Union County's Black Soldiers and Sailors of the Civil War,* the History Press, Charleston, S.C., 2011.

Wisnoski, Donald, *The Opportunity is at Hand; Oneida County, New York Colored Soldiers in the Civil War.* Lynchburg, Va.: Schroeder Publications, 2003.

NEWSPAPERS

Americus Recorder
Decatur Daily
Pittston Gazette
Sunday Independent
The Cincinnati Herald
The Cincinnati Enquirer
The Leader Herald
Washington Post

ELECTRONICS

Ancestry.com

en.wikepedia./org/wiki/John_Wayles_Jefferson

horsham.patch.com/groups/events/p/dedication-of-tombstone-on-grave-of-civil-war-veteran-barkley-stagner

http://emergingcivilwar.com/2011/11/21/african-americans-in-the-civil-war-part-2/

http://www.findagrave.com/cgi-n/fg.cgi?page=pv&GRid=5747861

http://www.itd.nps.gov/css/andDetailp.cfm

http://www.michiganinthewar.org/infantry/16compfk.htm

http://www.newyorkhistoryblog.com/2012/01/african-american-men-in-white-ny-civil-html

http://www.oberlin.edu/external/EOG/CivilWarTour/Stop2.html
http://www.pbs.org/wgbh/pages/frontline/shows/jefferson/cron/1902sprig.html
http://rustbeltradical.wordpress.com/tag/abolitionism

http://thecincinnatiherald.com/news/2013/oct/31/black-white-masons-mark-black-civil-vets-grave/

http://www.theintell.com/honoring-one-of-their-own/html_a7acbb2d-8407-570d-be39-2915ffbf9d2b.html

www.lwfaah.net

www.1stalabamacavalryusv.com

www.aaregistry.org/historic_events/view/abolitionist-william-h-johnson-born

www.usatoday.com/story/new/nation/2013/07/18/cemeteries-join-fight-to-mark-veterans-graves/2567209

Civil War Re-enactors
1st Alabama Cavalry and 13th U.S. Colored Troops Living Association
Pvt. Amos McKinney Memorial 11 July 2009
(Courtesy of Reba N. Burruss-Barnes)

Certificate of Special

Congressional Recognition

Presented to

Mrs. Juanita Patience Moss

in recognition of outstanding and invaluable service to the community.

July 11, 2009
DATE

MEMBER OF CONGRESS

Certificate of Special Congressional Recognition
From The Honorable Parker Griffith
Presented to Juanita Patience Moss
On the Occasion of the Pvt. Amos McKinney Memorial
On July 11, 2009
At Decatur, Alabama
(Courtesy of Peggy Allen Towns, Congressional Aide)

INDEX

<u>Discharge Record for Pvt. Crowder Patience</u>
103rd Pennsylvania Volunteers Co. C
A Compilation by Delanta Joseph Mills 2009
Descendants' Room
African American Civil War Museum
Washington, D.C.

Pvt. Amos McKinney Memorial
Magnolia-Sykes Cemetery
Decatur, Alabama
July 11, 2009

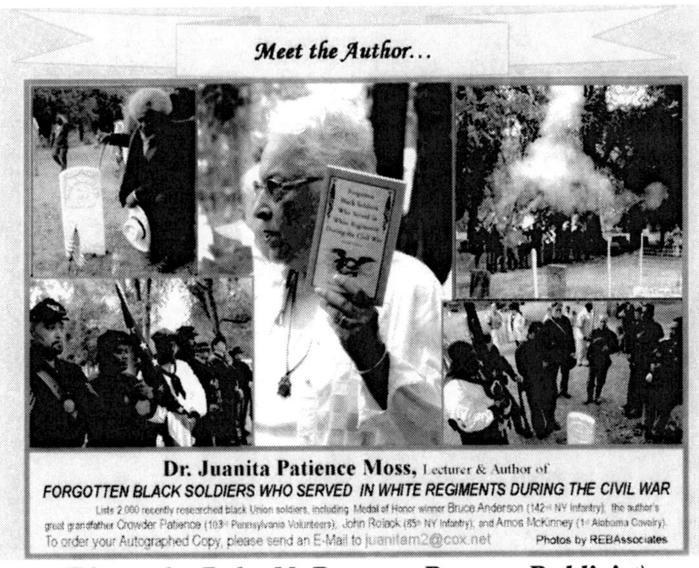

Meet the Author...
Dr. Juanita Patience Moss, Lecturer & Author of
FORGOTTEN BLACK SOLDIERS WHO SERVED IN WHITE REGIMENTS DURING THE CIVIL WAR
Lists 2,000 recently researched black Union soldiers, including Medal of Honor winner Bruce Anderson (142nd NY Infantry), the author's
great grandfather Crowder Patience (103rd Pennsylvania Volunteers), John Rolack (85th NY Infantry), and Amos McKinney (1st Alabama Cavalry).
To order your Autographed Copy, please send an E-Mail to juanitam2@cox.net
Photos by REBAssociates

(Photos by Reba N. Burruss-Barnes, Publicist)

ABOUT THE AUTHOR

JUANITA PATIENCE MOSS, born in northeastern Pennsylvania, graduated from the West Pittston Public School System; attended Bennett College in Greensboro, North Carolina; received a B.S. degree from Wilkes College, Wilkes-Barre, Pennsylvania; a M.A. degree from Fairleigh Dickinson University, Rutherford, New Jersey; and an Honorary Doctor of Humanities from Kings College, Wilkes-Barre, Pennsylvania. A retired New Jersey high school biology teacher, she developed an interest in genealogy that led to her researching Black soldiers whose service in white regiments had not been documented. Her great grandfather, Crowder Patience, who served in the 103rd Pennsylvania Volunteers, was one of them.

BOOKS BY DR. JUANITA PATIENCE MOSS

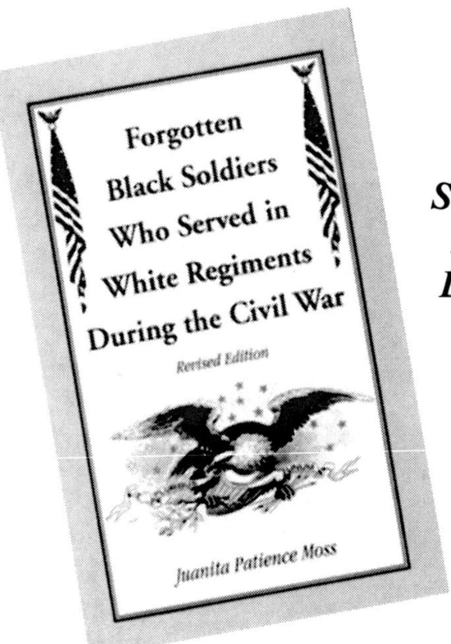

FORGOTTEN BLACK SOLDIERS WHO SERVED IN WHITE REGIMENTS DURING THE CIVIL WAR

Revised Version in 2008
IBSN: 978-0-7884-4647-4

This book traces the ten year odessy taken by the author as she set out to prove a hypothesis. She was told by historians and archivists that there had been no Black soldiers serving in white regiments when she knew of at least one—her great grandfather who had served in the 103rd Pennsylvania Volunteers and not in a segregated regiment.

Historians and Civil War "buffs" alike will find new information revealed in this book, even though 150 years have passed since the last shopt of the was was fired. Civil War history is still amazingly of great interest to many people. An index to full names, places ans juibjects adds to the value of this book.

CREATED TO BE FREE

IBSN: 1-58549-704-5

This historical novel is based on the life of an 18-year-old runaway slave who joined the 103rd Pennsylvania Regiment when it was garrisoned in Plymouth, N.C. The reason for writing the book was because several historians had told the author there had been no black men serving in white regiments during the Civil War.

The author's research led her to write about her ancestor's 83-year life journey from the sweet potato fields of North Carolina to the anthracite coal fields of northeastern Pennsylvania. Escaping from Chowan County, the slave boy Toby became the free man Crowder Pacien (Patience.)

This book is about one American family, in some ways different from all others, but in many ways mirroring many others because it is a story of tenacity and survival. There is something in this books for everyone, regarless of ethnicity.

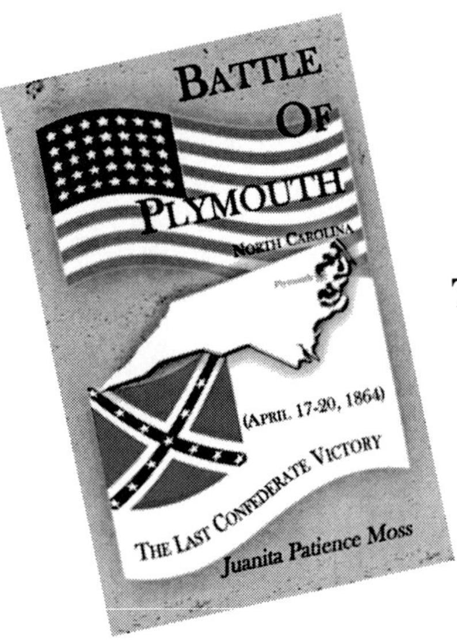

BATTLE OF PLYMOUTH, N.C.: APRIL 17-20, 1864 THE LAST CONFEDERATE VICTORY

ISBN: 1-58549-852-1

Many people have not heard about the Battle of Plymouth, even avid Civil War "buffs." Well, that's not surprising because very little has been written about it. Read this detailed and carefully researched book to learn about the second largest battle in North Carolina.

Intense drama took place during the four days filled with surprise, fate, intrigue, bravery, ingenuity, hope, daring, dedication, gallantry, victory for the Rebels and disappointment and defeat for the Yankees.

Thirteen Black soldiers were serving in four white regiments garrisoned there. These and others like them have been forgotten by historians. This book proves to modern nay-sayers that there were some Black soldiers in white regiments during the Civl War, the author's ancestor being one of them.

Have you heard of the CSS Albemarle, a ship built not in a shipyard as expected, but in a cornfield? Are you aware of who is credited with having achieved the most daring venture in all of the Civil War, and that it happened at Plymouth, North Carolina?

CPSIA information can be obtained
at www.ICGtesting.com
Printed in the USA
LVOW10s0848120218
566199LV00004B/351/P